A. Macnamara,

St Edward's School,
Oxford.

DISCARDED

THE
UNIVERSITY OF WINNIPEG
PORTAGE & BALMORAL
WINNIPEG 2. MAN.   CANADA

HENRY YEVELE

Some Press Opinions of this Book

". . . Mr. Harvey's scholarly, enthusiastic and beautifully illustrated book . . . as productive of thought as anything of Lethaby's; an adequate commentary on it might run to many volumes; it is a seminal summary of many elements in civilisation hung upon the peg of the career of one man's life.—SIR JOHN SQUIRE in *The Illustrated London News*.

"At long last . . . one of the greatest of our medieval architects, the head of his profession, the Wren of his age, and blessed like Wren with long life and opportunities of using his great gifts over many years, has been accorded a full-length biography, with numerous drawings and photographs to illustrate his works . . , The author and his publishers are to be congratulated on their imagination and enterprise in presenting in such attractive form the results of long and patient research."—ARTHUR OSWALD in *Country Life*.

"This is a fascinating book, written from an unusual angle . . . his story is a gripping one and his conclusions and inferences have percipience and force. It is impossible to conclude this review without placing on record the amount of enjoyment obtainable from . . . the well-chosen illustrations."—*The Architect and Building News*.

"Mr. Harvey's book, accurate, enthusiastic, fully documented and generously illustrated, is a long overdue tribute to one of this country's greatest architects, and also to the style of which he was such a master."—*The Spectator*.

"His book, with its wealth of fine illustrations, most skilfully related to the text, is a worthy tribute to a great Englishman."—*The Times Literary Supplement*.

". . . a book remarkable for its sympathy and scholarship." —*The Scotsman*.

"This original and readable book, with its seventy illustrations and its fascinating jacket designed by the author, is in the best Batsford tradition."—*The Birmingham Post*.

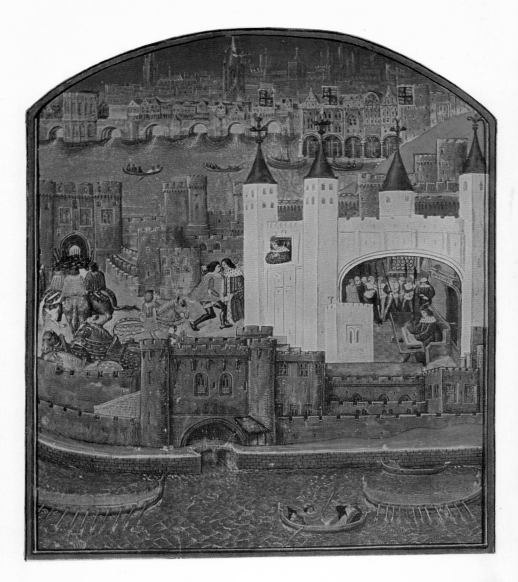

THE TOWER OF LONDON, BILLINGSGATE AND LONDON BRIDGE, ABOUT 1500.

From a MS. of the Poems of Charles Duke of Orleans, British Museum,
Royal MS. 16 F.11, fol. 73.

NA
997
.D4H3
1946

HENRY YEVELE

c. 1320 to 1400

The Life of an English Architect

By

JOHN H. HARVEY

LONDON
B. T. BATSFORD LTD.
15, NORTH AUDLEY STREET, W.1

The drawing on the title-page is of a misericord seat of c. 1365 from St. Katharine's-by-the-Tower, London, showing the head of a master craftsman of the period

First Published, Autumn, 1944
Second Edition, Spring, 1946

MADE AND PRINTED IN GREAT BRITAIN
FOR THE PUBLISHERS, B. T. BATSFORD LTD., LONDON
BY JARROLD AND SONS LTD., NORWICH

CONTENTS

For matter new to this Edition, see page 68

PREFACE

THIS IS NOT A BOOK FOR HISTORIANS OR ARCHAEOLOGISTS; IT IS A book for architects and the general public: at least for that part of the general public which does not shelter in caves or caravans, or climb into trees to sleep, but depends on architects for places to live in. For the benefit of anybody who is sufficiently interested to want references and authorities, there is a short bibliography at the end of the book.

The reader who wishes to deduce the moral (if any), should turn to Chapter V, where he will discover that I am advocating the study of the fourteenth century as a means of solving the problems of the twentieth, and especially the architectural problems. I am aware that there will be objections that the clock can't be put back, that the Gothic Revival was tried and failed, and that we can't bridge the gap between the outlook of Chaucer's time and that of our own day. To this I reply that the clock has to be put back when it is fast, that there never was a Gothic Revival, but only the exhumation and public exhibition of a mummy, and the gap between Chaucer and ourselves is several centuries less than it was in the days of our grandfathers, if I may be pardoned an Irishism.

The nineteenth century was less fitted to understand Gothic life than any period for some fifteen hundred years, but whatever we may think of the twentieth century, it has at any rate wiped the soapy grin off the face of Utopian Progress. Most people are being cured, rather drastically, of the hallucination that all previous periods were part of a steady progression towards the beatific vision of a machine age where the machines coin endless money for the sustenance of an all-knowing Enlightened Humanity. The Dark Ages, when corn was esteemed rather as a food, and even as a divine essence, than as an adjunct to the scenery for the benefit of the rambling townsman's half-holiday; when gold was considered so beautiful that it was worked by the hands of inspired artists into gifts for Kings, instead of being assiduously stored in reinforced and bomb-proof vaults, where no one, not even a King, can see it at all; when the senseless folly of personal combat between professional soldiers with a zest for fighting was preferred to the more magnificent spectacle of total war; these Dark Ages are again finding a few admirers, who are tempted to think that there was something in their spirit worth reviving, and that they possibly were not so dark after all.

There is a special reason why, out of those dark ages of past time, I choose the later part of the fourteenth century. It is the nearest period in English history when our culture, *as a whole*, was not visibly less balanced, less perfect, than what had gone before. I might have gone farther back, as a poet may seek his inspiration even from Virgil or Homer, or a sculptor from Phidias or his archaic predecessors. But to go farther back is to go beyond what is English; the history of all that we can distinguish from its French, Norman, Saxon, Danish, Celtic, or primitive Iberian component parts, begins about the thirteenth century and the process of transformation was only completed after the Black Death.

Architecturally, we have been in a mess for long enough, which is a polite way of saying too long. We have tried the principles of Vitruvius, that painstaking if uninspired Roman, the substitute principles of Palladio, the livelier fantasy of Wren, the massive solemnities of Vanbrugh, the stately classicism of Carr and the Woods, the Rococo delicacy of the Adam brothers, the pathetic imitations of Periclean Greece, and the Gothic Revival which was not very Gothic and anything but reviving. Since then there has been an era of the most amazing eclecticism which has ended in the blank despair of the so-called functionalist, whose purpose seems to be to strip life of all those apparently unessential graces which make life something more than existence.

Now it is not the slightest use in the world to get together a committee and proceed to found a new architecture on rational principles: we shall not get any masterpieces until a master has appeared in our midst. All the same, even a master has to add the hard-bought lessons of education and experience to the gifts of genius, and is bound to practise in a style which has some organic connection with the one in which he is brought up, even if it is only the connection of revolt. We are likely to need a great master, and many little masters, in the fairly near future, and now is the time to reconstitute architectural education, not in respect to method, but as to authority. Let us turn to the vital work of Henry Yevele and his colleagues, and see if they cannot teach us something about aesthetic values and even about real functionalism, which is the fitting of a building to its purpose in all aspects of that purpose, and not just the decorative aspects on the one hand, nor the material ones on the other.

Yevele had something to say on all sides of architecture, except perhaps town-planning, and even that omission may be a salutary warning to us. We may rightly condemn the narrow outlook which prevented Wren's town-plan of London being realised in practice, but not necessarily wish to live in New York or Buffalo rather than in London or Manchester. There is such a thing as too much planning like too much love or too much cake, and in avoiding the monster which lurks within the labyrinth, we should take care lest we suffer with St. Lawrence on the grid-iron.

In case anyone has begun to feel terrified that this is a Book with a Purpose, let me add that its chief aim is to bring to our remembrance the great life of one of the truest sons of England, who endowed us with several of the loveliest monuments of architecture, and who deserves our interest and affection, as well as the title of our greatest architect.

Much has been written on the subject of Henry Yevele during the past century, but the detailed research which has made possible this full-length biography is due mainly to the indefatigable labours of Professor Douglas Knoop and Mr. G. P. Jones; their results have been made known through the publications mentioned in the bibliography at the end of this book. I have to thank Professor Knoop and Mr. Jones for the very kind gift of copies of these publications, and for a great deal of other help, as well as for their permission to use the material for this biography.

For assistance in finding additional material and for helpful suggestions I am especially indebted to Mrs. Dorothy Gardiner; Dr. A. F. Pollard; Professor F. M. Stenton and the staff of the English Place-Name Society; Sir A. W. Clapham; and to Mr. C. J. P. Cave for his lovely photograph of the head from Canterbury Cloisters. I have also to thank the officials and staffs of the British Museum and Bodleian Libraries, the Public Record Office, the Library of the Royal Institute of British Architects, and the Society of Genealogists, and the following persons who have given assistance on special points:—

Mr. T. D. Atkinson, The Rt. Hon. H. T. Baker, The Rev. G. Montagu Benton, Mr. G. H. Chettle, The Lady Conway, The Rev. Norman Edwards, Mr. F. G. Emmison, Major F. N. Fisher, Mr. Joseph Fowler, Mr. S. J. Garton, Miss Joyce Godber, Mr. Walter H. Godfrey, Mr. John Goodchild, Mr. Aubrey Goodes, Mr. R. P. Howgrave-Graham, Sir Edward Harrison, Col. P. E. Hodgson, Dr. Wilfrid Hooper, Mr. H. A. James, Mr. John D. Knight, Dr. N. B. Lewis, Mr. A. W. McClellan, Miss L. M. Midgley, Mr. C. D. Miller, Mr. A. Vivian Neal, Mr. Bernard Rackham, Mr. L. F. Salzman, The Rev. E. St. G. Schomberg, Dr. W. Douglas Simpson, Mr. Austin Smyth, Mr. R. Somerville, Mr. W. P. D. Stebbing, Mr. John Summerson, Dom Thomas Symons, Mr. Lawrence E. Tanner, Dr. A. H. Thomas, Mr. H. J. Wasbrough, and others whose names now escape me, but whose remarks or suggestions have here borne fruit.

I have also to express my special gratitude to Mr. Harry Batsford for the enthusiasm he has poured into the illustration of the book, and to Mr. Charles Fry for his energetic work on the exacting and often exasperating details of its production. Finally, I must record my warm sense of indebtedness to my wife for her exemplary patience in listening, and for her help in matters of presentation, to my father William Harvey, to Mr. Herbert Chitty, and to Mr. E. A. Greening Lamborn for the help and encouragement they have given me, and to my friends Arthur Oswald and Ralph Davis, whose conversations and correspondence have done so much to fashion the view of architectural development sketched here.

HALF MOON COTTAGE,   JOHN H. HARVEY
    LITTLE BOOKHAM, SURREY
19 *February*, 1944

A NOTE ON THE ILLUSTRATIONS

Dates given under illustrations indicate the approximate year of design

The frontispiece shows the Tower of London about 1500. The thatched awning against the right-hand turret of the Traitor's Gate was one of the sheds used by the Office of Works. In the background is London Bridge, with the Chapel of St. Thomas as rebuilt by Yevele *c.* 1384; on the right are the arcaded warehouses of Billingsgate. Between these and the Bridge lay the church of St. Magnus and Yevele's home. The boats on the river catered for a large proportion of London's passenger transport, including the journey of royal officials from Westminster to the Tower and City. (*From Royal MS.* 16 *F.* 11, *fol.* 73, *by kind permission of the Trustees of the British Museum.*)

The vignette on the title-page shows a royal master craftsman (possibly Henry Yevele, see p. 78) of *c.* 1365, from a misericord seat transferred to St. Katharine's Hospital, Regent's Park, after the demolition of St. Katharine's-by-the-Tower.

Figs. 2, 24, 35, 50, 51, and 61 are after drawings and engravings by, or based on Hollar; details of the originals will be found in Arthur M. Hind: *Wenceslaus Hollar and his Views of London*, 1922.

Figs. 7, 12, 13, and 14 are taken from Pepysian MS. 1916 at Magdalene College, Cambridge, reproduced in Vol. XIII of the Walpole Society, 1925, Plates XVII, XX, XXI, XXII. The MS. is an artist's sketch-book and contains the work of several hands, *c.* 1400 or later, but the architectural drawings (Figs. 7, 13, 14) are rather earlier, and have been mutilated by re-cutting the parchment to form the book. Probably a monastic artist made himself a sketch-book out of unwanted sheets of parchment from the Master Mason's tracing office. Many architectural drawings were made in the Middle Ages, but these are practically all that survive in England of a date earlier than 1450.

Figs. 19, 20 are from the late Canon H. F. Westlake's *Westminster Abbey*, 2 vols., 1923.

Fig. 25 is from a sketch by Antony van den Wyngaerde in Bodleian MS. Sutherland 171, f. 11. It is dated 1562, while another view apparently made at nearly the same time shows the site of the ruined hall cleared. This sketch, and a smaller copy in Wyngaerde's finished view of Richmond Palace from the waterside (Sutherland 171, f. 12) are the only authorities for any part of the pre-Tudor Palace of Shene, destroyed by fire in 1498.

Figs. 42–45 are taken from the only surviving roll of Wykeham's Household Accounts, preserved among the archives of Winchester College. Though the initials of the guests are only given occasionally, most of them have been identified from other sources by Mr. Herbert Chitty, F.S.A. In the seven months of 1393 covered by the roll, Yevele was a guest on 29th of April, 5th, 9th, 15th of May, 15th, 21st, 22nd, 29th of June, and 3rd of July; on all these dates it appears probable that Wykeham was in Southwark. Hugh Herland, who lived at Kingston-on-Thames, visited Wykeham at Esher on 28th of May and 11th of June, and at Winchester on 26th, 27th, and 31st of July, 21st, 22nd, and 24th of August, and 14th of September, while Wynford was a guest on 24th, 26th, 27th, and 31st of July, 3rd, 10th, 15th, 21st, 22nd, 24th, and 31st of August, and 7th and 14th of September.

Fig. 46 is from a French MS. of the late fourteenth century, the *Bible Historiale de Charles VI et du Duc de Berry*, and distinguishes clearly between the Master Mason who is directing the work, and the several categories of building craftsmen.

Fig. 47, from British Museum MS. Roy. 2 B. VII, is valuable for its view of a drawing board, with what may be intended for a full-size setting-out of voussoirs for an arch or vault.

Fig. 48 shows the figures of the Winchester College architectural staff in 1393, from the East window of the College Chapel. The glass is an early nineteenth-century copy, but is a very accurate reproduction of the original so far as draughtsmanship is concerned. In the same window is also a figure of Thomas the Glass-painter. For further details see J. D. Le Couteur: *Ancient Glass in Winchester*, 1920.

Fig. 54 is from an aquatint by Joseph Farington, R.A., in Boydell's *History of the River Thames*. Other views, with a detailed history of the bridge, are to be found in M. J. Becker: *Rochester Bridge*, 1930.

Fig. 63 is reproduced from the late Lord Curzon's monograph, *Bodiam Castle*.

The author and publishers here express their indebtedness to the following persons for the illustrations mentioned: Miss Margaret Babington, O.B.E., and the Friends of Canterbury Cathedral for Fig. 18; Bodley's Librarian for Figs. 25, 35; the Trustees of the British Museum for Fig. 1; Mr. C. J. P. Cave, F.S.A. for Fig. 40; Central Press Photos for Fig. 69; Mr. John Charlton, Canterbury, for Fig. 64; Sir A. W.Clapham, P.S.A., for Figs. 22 (from *Some Famous Buildings*), 30; Country Life, Ltd. for Figs. 29, 37, 39, 68; Mr. Fred. H. Crossley, F.S.A., for Figs. 10, 34, 52; Mr. E. Dockree for Fig. 33; Mr. Herbert Felton, F.R.P.S., for Figs. 26, 66, 70; Sir Banister Fletcher for Fig. 56 (from *A History of Architecture*); Mr. Walter H. Godfrey, F.S.A., for Fig. 57 (from *A History of Architecture in London*, 1911); H.M. Stationery Office for Fig. 49 (from the Blue Book on *Westminster Hall*, 1914); the Kent Archaeological Society for Fig. 32 (from *Archaeologia Cantiana*, Vol. XI); Mr. A. F. Kersting for Figs. 5, 15, 55; Mr. W. F. Mansell for Fig. 11; The National Buildings Record for Figs. 4, 58, 70; the Royal Commission on Historical Monuments (England) for Figs. 8, 53, 59, 65 (from *Westminster Abbey*) and Fig. 23 (from *London, West*); Messrs. Walter Scott, Bradford, for Fig. 17; Mr. Will. F. Taylor for Figs. 6, 9, 16, 27, 36, 38, 41, 60, 71; Messrs. J. Tiranti & Co. for Fig. 28 (from *Westminster Abbey and St. Margaret's Church*, 1920); Mr. Sidney Toy, F.S.A., and the Royal Archaeological Institute for Fig. 32 (from *Archaeological Journal*, Vol LXXXVI); the Walpole Society for Figs. 7, 12, 13, 14 (from Walpole Soc., Vol. XIII, 1924–25); and the Warden and Fellows of Winchester College for Figs. 42–45 (photographer Mr. G. H. Salmon), and Fig. 48 (photographer, Mr. Sydney Pitcher, F.R.P.S.). The vignette on title-page, and Figs. 7, 21, 31, 67 are from line drawings by the author.

INTRODUCTION

SO FAR AS I KNOW, NO ENGLISH ARCHITECT OF THE MIDDLE AGES has yet been thought worthy of a full-length biography, and only two have articles in the Dictionary of National Biography, one of whom is the subject of the present essay. Henry Yevele has been recognised for a century as the principal architectural figure in those "dark" ages about which so much has been written, and which yet seem to the average man very remote. Architecturally, this ought not to be the case, for the buildings of the Middle Ages in England were the result of centuries of growing tradition, which was strong enough to absorb the external influences brought by the Normans and the Crusaders, and thus to develop as a true national style. Architecture since 1550, on the contrary, has been a product of foreign origin, rather clumsily grafted on to the English plan and structure, or during the period of the Gothic revival, generally unintelligent copying of mediaeval forms in unsympathetic materials and entirely without the vital spark of a live tradition. So it comes about that modern England thinks of Inigo Jones and Sir Christopher Wren as the pre-eminently great English architects, though they worked in a foreign style as yet imperfectly assimilated to English tradition.

English architecture, properly so-called, developed out of the Saxon buildings of pre-Conquest times, and was profoundly modified by the French Romanesque traditions which were imported by Edward the Confessor, and later imposed upon the country by the Norman Conquest. Saxon England possessed, before the Danish invasions, a culture of great magnificence, and even after the disastrous wars of the ninth-eleventh centuries, the wealth of London and the rich clothing of the Saxon nobles impressed the Continent. But England had become a backwater, and we owe to William the Conqueror the fact that the northern island again became a part of the European system. The King of England was also an important prince in right of his French possessions, and the royal marriages linked England to all the great cultural centres of the western world.

Soon after the Norman Conquest the Crusades took Kings, nobles, and large bodies of men from western Europe to the Levant, and a proportion of them returned, bringing with them the germs of an architectural style quite distinct from the Romanesque of the eleventh and early twelfth centuries. Such Saracenic works as the Dome of the Rock in Jerusalem must have made a great impression upon the cultured Europeans who saw them for the first time, and the pointed arch, of very ancient standing in the East, was introduced to the West. The pointed arch rendered possible the further development of the groined vault, and simultaneously a great improvement took place in the technique of the building crafts. Smoothly dressed ashlar masonry with fine joints was capable of bearing far greater loads and resisting greater thrusts than the coarse older work had been, and the new skill must have been rapidly improved by a selective process. This process was to

go on for the next four centuries, the King exercising his power of impressment to secure the finest craftsmen for his service, and the great nobles and
ecclesiastics doing the same within their own spheres of influence.

Local traditions grew up in some districts, sometimes round stone quarries,
but generally connected with one of the greater monastic houses, which were
constantly building and rebuilding through the whole period, and had a
staff of artists and artisans in residence. At the same time there was one
other school of even greater importance: that attached to the King's Court at
Westminster, where the permanent administration centred. The King was
not always in residence at Westminster, but spent a large proportion of his
life moving from place to place, carrying with him the whole immense
apparatus of the Royal Household. At certain points he could live in his
own castles and manor-houses, at others he was the guest of a monastery,
but all the time he was dealing with local problems and seeing with his own
eyes just what was going on in all parts of the country. Promising artists
discovered during these progresses went to swell the numbers of the "office
of works" centred at Westminster. Thus it came about that a truly national
architecture developed under royal patronage, and acquired men of genius
from all parts of the realm.

The headquarters of the King's works was at Westminster, in the great
Palace over against the Abbey, but some departments were housed in the
Tower of London, and there were other sections in charge of such great
buildings as Windsor Castle. Topography played a considerable part in the
formation of contacts between the royal and local schools. The closest links
were those which bound Westminster to London, its great commercial
neighbour; to Canterbury, "the Mother of England", and Dover, with their
royal castles on the route to the Continent; to Winchester the ancient Saxon
capital, with another royal castle; and to Windsor and the upper Thames
Valley. By the last route London was connected with Gloucester and Bristol,
both great centres of trade and seats of important abbeys and royal castles.
Gloucester and Bristol Abbeys alone provided much work for masons, and
so did several of the other large monasteries of the west, notably Bath,
Cirencester, Tewkesbury, and Winchcombe. Of these six great abbeys we
have considerable remains of three, Bristol, Gloucester, and Tewkesbury,
but the others are totally destroyed, and it is probable that some of the most
important links in our artistic development have disappeared with them.
Enough still remains to make possible some account of the progress of style
in England, and the names of many of the greatest architects survive.

The first clear example of the transition from Romanesque to Gothic is
found in the work of William of Sens at Canterbury Cathedral. Master
William was invited to come from France to carry out the work, and the new
choir is thus a French building erected in England. William of Sens was,
however, severely injured by falling from a scaffold after the first three years'
work, (1175–1178) and his assistant, William the Englishman, took charge
of the construction of the Trinity Chapel and Corona (Becket's Crown),
finished in 1184. This work is much further removed from the Romanesque

style than the choir of Sens' design, and from this point the Gothic style was rapidly developed in English hands. The reconstruction of 1187–1199 at Chichester was in the style of William Englishman's work at Canterbury, and may well have been designed by him, and between 1192 and 1200 Geoffrey de Noyers built the choir and eastern transepts at Lincoln for St. Hugh. This is the earliest known building of pure Gothic design, not only in England, but in the world; its details, though influenced by the new work of Canterbury, are thoroughly English, and do not resemble any French work of the same or earlier periods. De Noyers was doubtless of French extraction, but his immediate forbears seem to have been settled in Lincolnshire for some time. For nearly two generations English Gothic developed steadily, the leading influence being that of Lincoln, where Master Alexander followed de Noyers as cathedral architect.

It was at this period that the primacy of style fell into the hands of the royal school, where it was to remain for the last three centuries of English Gothic art. The reason for this lay in the growing taste of Henry III, the most art-loving King who ever sat upon the throne of England, save Richard II, and while Richard's adult rule lasted only ten years, that of Henry counted a half-century. In the early years of Henry's reign, a prominent architectural influence was that of Elias de Derham. Derham was a clerk in the royal service, and the extent of his reliance upon the technical knowledge of the master craftsmen is unknown, but whether direct or indirect, Derham's influence was responsible for the design of Salisbury Cathedral, begun in 1220, the West Front of Wells Cathedral, the great hall of Winchester Castle, begun about 1232, and the Chapel of the Nine Altars at Durham, started about 1242. Derham died in 1245, but his position in regard to the King's works became less important in the last years of his life, and the great period of royal work which began about 1239 was in the hands of Master Henry de Reyns, the greatest master mason of the time. Master Henry's origin has never been cleared up, and the evidence is of the kind which suggests almost as many theories as there are students of the problem. The indisputable facts are these: "Henry master of the King's masons" was granted a robe by the King's order on the 10th of December, 1243, the same order including a robe for William le Brun, keeper of the works at Windsor Castle. In the following year Master Henry was sent to York to look to the defences of the castle there, and in 1245 began the rebuilding of the church and chapter house of Westminster Abbey, which were certainly designed by him. Lethaby showed that the details of the King's Chapel at Windsor Castle begun in 1239, were practically identical with those of Westminster, so that it is safe to say that Master Henry was chief architect at least as early as the late 1230's. All his detail is of English character, yet the general design of Westminster follows French models very closely, and the inspiration was undoubtedly the newly built cathedral of Rheims, whose original design, including the bar-traceried windows, goes back to c. 1212. The fact that "Reyns," Master Henry's surname, was the common English spelling for Rheims, is a most extraordinary coincidence, if it does not indicate some connection between the French Coronation Church, and the architect of the English one. It is true that certain places in England were also spelt Reyns at the same period, but *the* Reyns *par excellence* was that in France. It does not seem to have been suggested that Master Henry, though of English origin and training, may have worked at Rheims, and on his return was known by a new surname, a proceeding which would then be quite normal. To me this seems the only probable solution for it reconciles all the known facts without straining our credulity with coincidences, and amply explains the intimate knowledge of French work which the architect of Westminster obviously possessed. The new abbey church was, in fact, the precursor of the Geometrical style in England, a style which was immediately diffused by the King's architects and those of the greater religious houses. Probably the earliest steps in this diffusion were at the abbeys of Hayles and Netley; Hayles was founded in 1246 by Richard King of the Romans, Henry III's brother, while Netley, founded in 1239, under the will of Peter des Roches, Bishop of Winchester, was taken under the royal patronage by Henry III in 1251, after which the greater part of the work was carried out. Both these houses were Cistercian, and in consequence were built in a simplified version of the new style, to fulfil the severe rules of the order.

The introduction of bar-tracery from France by Master Henry about 1240 constituted the last debt of English Gothic to the Continent; henceforward the insular architecture was to develop internally until the acceptance of Renaissance detail killed the native product. One further borrowing did take place, though in planning, not in style; this was the conception of the concentric castle, introduced by Edward I on his return from the Crusade in 1274.[1] At Westminster, Master Henry had been succeeded in 1253 by John of Gloucester, who died in 1260, being followed by his assistant Robert of Beverley. Master Robert probably came from the works of the great northern minster whose High Altar was consecrated in 1260, marking the completion of the choir and transepts. In 1271 Robert had become surveyor of the King's works, and on Edward I's return it was Master Robert who took charge of the new works at the Tower of London, which transformed it into a "concentric" castle, with the addition of a series of strong gate-towers and a barbican to guard the main entrance. Robert of Beverley died in 1284, but before his death several other royal architects were coming into prominence. Of these, Master James of St. George seems to have been a foreigner, perhaps a Frank born in Palestine, and engaged purely as a military expert. His colleague in the building of the great series of castles in North Wales, Master Richard Lenginour, was also, as his name recalls, an engineer in the first instance, though he appears also to have worked for St. Werburgh's Abbey in Chester, whose church survives as the present cathedral. The third of a great triumvirate of castle-builders was Walter of Hereford, the architect of Carnarvon Castle (1285–1315). Master Walter, unlike his two colleagues, was not a military engineer by training, but a mason with experience of

---

[1] Modern authorities, following Professor William Rees, consider that the concentric works of Caerphilly Castle are probably later than 1271, when work on the castle had begun.

first-class church work, having become master of the new works of Winchcombe Abbey in 1278, and later in the same year being appointed to the office of master at the building of Vale Royal Abbey in Cheshire, founded by Edward I. From building this great abbey he went on to Carnarvon, but he travelled to other parts of the country, being at Edinburgh Castle in 1304, during the English occupation, and two years later taking masons to London for "the Queen's work." This work was the building of the Grey Friars' Church in Newgate for Margaret, the second Queen of Edward I. In this great friary church were found fully developed the new tendencies in English church design: the transepts had disappeared, and the church was practically one great hall, divided into three aisles by arcades, and well lighted with large windows.

From a solid building pierced with small holes for light, the church had become a glass-house supported and roofed by means of slender uprights, the whole structure being knit together by perfect construction. Walter of Hereford was undoubtedly the greatest architect in general practice around the turn of the century, but he was ably seconded by several other members of the royal school, notably John of Battle who had been his assistant at Vale Royal, and was one of the designers of the Eleanor Crosses, built in 1291–1294, and Richard Crundale, who also worked on the Eleanor Crosses, and the tomb of Queen Eleanor in Westminster Abbey. Crundale was probably from Kent, and several other important Westminster masons were from Canterbury, during the succeeding half-century. The work of this school penetrated even to the north of England, for Edward I refounded the town of Hull in 1296, and the great church of Holy Trinity there was laid out on a plan almost as advanced as that of the London Grey Friars ten years later; the resemblances in scale and planning are so close that Walter of Hereford must be suspected as the architect at Hull, and he certainly was the most likely of the royal craftsmen to have been employed at a place where problems of town-planning, fortification, and religious architecture were being tackled simultaneously.

The reign of Edward I closed the thirteenth century and extended a few years beyond it, but comparatively little architectural work was going on in the concluding years of the reign, probably owing to the repeated Scottish wars. There was, in fact, a slight but marked pause, roughly corresponding to the division between the Geometric and Curvilinear periods of the Decorated style. The work begun by Henry de Reyns before 1250 was completed by Walter of Hereford, who did not die until 1315, and the result was to give England a flourishing native architecture which was actually more advanced in character than that of France, or any other continental country. The campaigns and legal reforms of Edward I had succeeded in giving security to the whole country except the extreme north, and a new type of unfortified or only slightly defended manor-house was coming into being as a result. Now that the stern necessities of defence were passing away, there was room for additional offices and for greatly enlarged living apartments.

The old aisled hall with its rows of oak posts (or occasionally stone columns), gave place to an open span roofed by wide trusses capable of omitting both posts and tie-beams. The open preaching churches of the Friars also required trussed timber roofs, and there was consequently a great development in roof construction regarded as an experimental science. This new science of timber roofing had no parallel abroad; mediaeval England produced timber roofs of vastly greater importance than those of any other country, regarded both structurally and aesthetically. Lastly, the greater and parochial churches alike had been affected by the demand for light and preaching-space, and the "dim religious light" which filtered through the rich early glass set in narrow lancet windows now gave place to a brilliant glory of sunshine which lit up the whole building and made it necessary to provide the walls and vaults with enrichments, so that this flood of light might be broken up, and made to yield patterns of light and shade.

Among the earliest examples of lierne vaults is that of the crypt of St. Stephen's Chapel in Westminster Palace, finished in 1327 by Master Walter of Canterbury. A lierne vault, in the sense understood in this country, is one which contains subsidiary ribs which are neither structural ribs springing from the walls or piers, nor ridge-ribs, but cross from one main rib to another, forming stellar and other patterns. Tracery was applied to wall-surfaces, and internally little plain walling would be left, while outside there were niches for statues, elaborate gablets and pinnacles on the buttresses, and pierced parapets with cusped openings showing against the sky.

These tendencies towards elaboration broke loose after the death of Walter of Hereford, and new experiments such as filling hollow mouldings with the ball-flower ornament were tried; these, and many of the more extreme instances of decorative work of an "appliqué" character, resulted in a surfeit of good things, and much of the work of the second quarter of the fourteenth century degenerated into a riot of exquisitely carved ornament applied without restraint. Another sign of falling-off was the extreme naturalism of the floral motives so largely used. This last division of the Decorated period was beginning to show a real failure of inspiration, a failure well displayed in the choir-vault of Gloucester Cathedral (then Abbey), designed in the 1340's, where the ingenuity of the craftsman was the undoing of the artistic result, and the eye cannot follow the beauty of the patterns on account of the superabundance of lierne ribs. This luxuriant art reflected the effeminacy of the court of Edward II, and just as a series of political revolutions led to the reign of Edward III, so an artistic revolution, slightly delayed, was to bring in the last Gothic style as an artistic background to the noble magnificence of this King's reign.

The political disturbances which closed the reign of Edward II, and the minority of his son, led to another pause in architectural activity, lasting from about 1325 to 1330, though this did not interfere with works already in progress. The Chapel of St. Stephen in the Palace of Westminster was at last begun, after the completion of its basement or crypt, in 1327, and the architect of the upper chapel was Master Thomas of Canterbury, probably son of Walter, and perhaps grandson of Master Michael of Canterbury, under whom the crypt had been started in 1292. The upper chapel, which was

2 London, Old St. Paul's: Chapter House and Cloister, 1332. Designer: William Ramsey; from an engraving after Hollar. The first known Perpendicular building; for drawings and description see R. H. C. Finch: Old St. Paul's, in *The Builder*, 19th and 26th April, 1935

3 Ely Cathedral: Octagon from North-west. 1322; 1334
Designers: Master John; John atte Grene

4 Ely Cathedral: Lantern, looking up. *c*. 1334
Designer: William Hurley

not structurally completed until after 1345, was one of the supreme master-pieces of English art: fortunately its enrichment was largely a matter of colour decoration, and the design followed Geometric rather than Curvilinear precedents. Aisleless, it had two storeys of windows and a timber vault, and was a perfect example of the new "glass-house" construction. Above the windows the spandrels of walling were filled in with a panelling of vertical ribs and cusped heads of geometrical type. This vertical panelling gave a definite hint of the "Perpendicular" treatment of walls, a hint which was to be seized on by one of Thomas of Canterbury's assistants, William de Ramsey, and by William Hurley the carpenter, who also worked with Master Thomas at St. Stephen's Chapel, and at the London Guildhall Chapel from 1332.

The credit for the invention of what we know as the Perpendicular style belongs to William de Ramsey, or perhaps to Ramsey and Hurley jointly. The critical change in moulding profiles only came gradually of course, but the new ideas of pattern were devised by Ramsey and Hurley, and applied to buildings of the first rank well before the Black Death. Ramsey was invited to design the new Chapter House and Cloister of St. Paul's Cathedral in London, and he was actually engaged in the supervision of the work by the summer of 1332. The buildings themselves perished in the Great Fire of 1666, but Hollar's fine engraving clearly shows the new detail, including the vertical panel treatment in the spandrels of the basement arches of the chap-ter-house, and some entirely fresh types of window-tracery, linked to the "long-panel" bay design, in which the window-mullions are carried down-wards over a space of blank wall. Over the lower cloister arches is a band of quatrefoils contained between vertical ribs. The chapter-house windows are reticulated, but the net is that of wire-netting, so that the cusped lights in the head are bounded by straight lines instead of flowing stems (2).

Meanwhile, another remarkable work was in progress at Ely Cathedral, where the Norman central tower had fallen in 1322, and was being replaced by an octagon, with the immense span of 68 feet. As far up as the heads of the great windows in the diagonal sides, this octagon is Curvilinear work of very fine type indeed, but showing no tendencies whatever towards Per-pendicular. This was completed about 1328, and a pause ensued on account of the difficulty of roofing this great open space. Evidently neither Alan of Walsingham the sacrist, nor John the master mason, was capable of surmount-ing this problem. In the end Master William Hurley was called in from London about 1334, and a new mason, John atte Grene, appeared at Ely. By 1342 Hurley had completed a wooden vault and lantern, and John atte Grene, who was master mason at Ely at least as early as 1339, had added to the stone octagon an upper storey, pierced by lights whose mullions ran through to a flat head, the top of each light being formed of ogee ribs with cinque-foil cusping. Above a string-course the vertical lines of the mullions con-tinued in the parapet. Hurley's wooden lantern contains even more marked Perpendicular treatment: externally, the blind openings above the windows are separated by mullions running up to the horizontal string beneath the cresting, and within, the space between the apex of the main timber vault

3

and the sills of the lantern windows is filled with vertical panelling. The base of the panelling is occupied by the motive of quatrefoils in squares, which Ramsey was using at St. Paul's, and the ribs ran upwards to form the main panelling; the head of each panel is filled with tracery which combines flowing and ogee lines with the new hexagonal reticulations (3, 4, 5).

Now all the inventions utilised by Ramsey in London and by Hurley at Ely were also being employed at Gloucester Abbey, where a great scheme of rebuilding, or rather recasing, was started in or after 1331. This work owed its inception to the burial of the murdered King Edward II in the Abbey in 1327, though during the domination of the country by Mortimer no overt steps to encourage the cult of the martyred King could be taken. Everything was changed by the fall of Mortimer at the end of 1330, when the young Edward III regained his kingdom and at once began to reorganise the conduct of affairs. He also promoted the veneration paid to his father's shrine, and there can be little doubt that William Ramsey, the genius in the royal service, was lent to Gloucester to provide designs for the transformation of the abbey church into a royal mortuary chapel. It would be a most extraordinary coincidence if this were not the case, for the Gloucester work includes such minutiae as the bands of quatrefoils so characteristic of the work of Ramsey and Hurley, with the new arrangement of the intermediate divisions prolonged to form tall vertical panels. The new window tracery was simply a further variation from the forms used at St. Paul's, and the four-centred arch was employed both there and at Gloucester. Though not an entirely new invention, the extensive use of four-centred arches with the upper arcs almost straight is characteristic of early Perpendicular work. The new work at Gloucester must in any case have been designed by a mason from outside, as it is totally different from the new south aisle of the nave, which had just been finished in 1329 (6).

Edward III had begun the reorganisation of the works by the appointment of Walter de Weston as Clerk of the Works in January 1331, and Robert de Hillum was granted the office of Comptroller in the following year. Finally, on the 1st June 1336 the establishment was reconstituted by the appointment of William Ramsey and Hurley as chief mason and carpenter respectively, and Walter le Fevre as chief smith. About this time the experimental work in the south transept of Gloucester was being finished, and it is probably significant that the next year saw a definite beginning made on the transformation of the choir there, while Ramsey was also called in by the canons of Lichfield Cathedral, to advise upon the works of their new presbytery (10). While Ramsey and Hurley were able to accept work for private clients, this certainly does not imply that no royal works were in progress, for not only was St. Stephen's Chapel still giving a great deal of employment, but the King began his vast project of rebuilding Windsor Castle. Ramsey and Hurley spent the whole year 1344 at Windsor, in charge of the building of an immense circular hall, 200 feet in diameter, the "Round Table." Unfortunately the work was abandoned, and nothing is known as to its design, but the fact that Ramsey had been building an octagonal chapter house, and Hurley a great

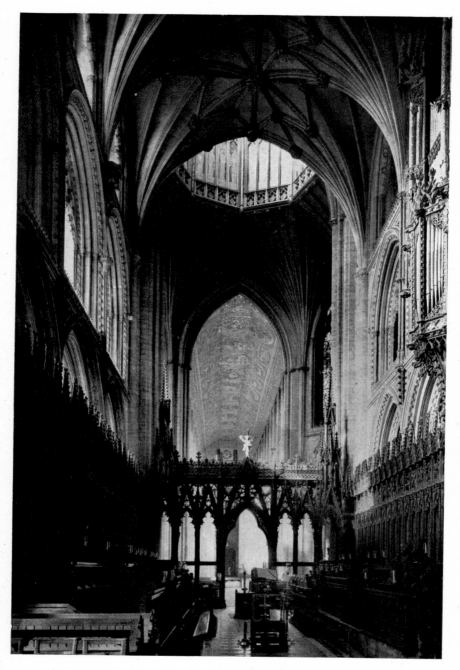

5 Ely Cathedral: Octagon vault and base of Lantern, *c.* 1334
Designer: William Hurley

6 Gloucester Cathedral: Presbytery looking North-east.
Recasing of 1337. Designer: possibly William Ramsey

octagonal vault and lantern, would lend colour to the idea that a large vaulted chamber surrounded by aisles must have been intended, to be roofed and lit by methods analogous to those employed by the architects elsewhere.

There was, however, a falling-off in the number of new works initiated during the 1340's, particularly at the greater churches, though this may be accounted for in part by the great quantity of work begun about 1330, which was still in progress. It is remarkable all the same that the Black Death of 1349 did not, as is generally stated, lead to a complete cessation of architectural work; on the contrary, many new building schemes were started between 1350 and 1355, including the great works at Windsor Castle, the new abbey of St. Mary Eastminster in London, Edington Priory in Wiltshire, Corpus Christi College and Trinity Hall, Cambridge, and the south and west cloisters of Westminster Abbey (8). But the Plague did mark a turning-point, for 1349 saw the deaths of William Ramsey, his brother John, also an important mason in the royal service, and Walter le Bole master mason to Westminster Abbey, though Hurley lived on until 1354. To fill the gaps in the royal establishment, John atte Grene was brought from Ely, John Box from Canterbury Cathedral, and the new buildings at Windsor Castle were put into the hands of John de Sponlee, who probably came from Spoonley near Winchcombe in Gloucestershire, and may have been the master mason of Winchcombe Abbey. Two Gloucester masons also entered the King's service, Thomas of Gloucester becoming warden of the masons at the Tower of London by 1354, and Robert of Gloucester having a similar post at Windsor Castle from about 1357.

There was no sudden spreading of the new style after 1350, and in some instances, as at Edington Priory, the Perpendicular elements of design appeared in buildings whose mouldings, and much of whose tracery, was still Decorated in character. It is noteworthy, however, that within the royal works the style was comparatively free from such admixture, and the buildings in Windsor Castle erected under John Sponlee between 1350 and 1356 are the first which belong quite definitely to the Perpendicular style, rather than to the period of transition (9).

Before 1360 the revolution had been accomplished, though in the more remote parts of the country Curvilinear designs appeared until the end of the century; the splendid tracery of the east window of Carlisle Cathedral, the finest of the style still in existence, having been built between 1363 and 1382. These belated Decorated works show that conservatism fought shy of the newcomer for some time, and this was not altogether without reason. The new choir of Gloucester, full of possibilities, had nevertheless failed to realise them, and appears wiry and empty when compared with the best works of the outgoing style. The new fashion had been devised, but not mastered, and many patrons of art must have been reluctant to find money for costly experiments, so long as the final effect was in doubt. Only the appearance of Perpendicular masterpieces would be convincing, and for the making of masterpieces the first requisite is a master. The master, a truly great one, was at hand, and his name was Henry Yevele.

Chapter I
Early Life and Surrounding Influences

THERE IS HARDLY ANY DIRECT EVIDENCE CONCERNING THE BIRTH and upbringing of Henry Yevele, but from the known facts of his later life a few assumptions may be permitted. He was already one of the most important masons in London at the beginning of 1356, and his "great age" is mentioned in 1390; on the other hand, he was still in practice and fairly active as late as 1396 and did not die until 1400. He is hardly likely to have been less than sixty-five in 1390, nor over ninety at the time of his death; and it is therefore safe to put the date of his birth in the near neighbourhood of 1320.

From his will it is known that his parents' Christian names were Roger and Marion, but there is no clue to their residence; later documents do however show that the Robert de Yevele, who was warden of the masons at the Tower of London from 1362, was Henry's brother, and this makes it extremely probable that their father also had been a mason. Yevele's birthplace, or at least the origin of his family, must have been "Yevele," for several references, including that of 1356, describe him as "de Yevele" or "de Yeevelee." Other spellings are *Yeveley* and *Zeveley*, and *Yvele, Iveleghe*, and *Zyveley*; (spellings with mediaeval "z" are simply variants from "g" or "y".) The suggested identifications which have been made include Yeovil, Somerset; Yeaveley, Derbyshire; Iffley, near Oxford; and Aveley in Essex, where Henry Yevele owned property.

After comparison of the forms in which Henry Yevele's name occurs, Professor F. M. Stenton concludes[1] that Yeaveley in Derbyshire is the only known place which satisfies the conditions, and this is fully borne out by the subsequent discovery that a "Roger de Zeveleye" and a "Geoffrey de Zeveleye" each paid 18*d*. to the subsidy of 1327, when they were living at Uttoxeter, Staffordshire, about seven miles from Yeaveley.[2] No other persons of this surname occur in the 1327 lists in Derbyshire or Staffordshire. It is reasonable to assume that this Roger de Zeveleye was the father of Henry and Robert, and though there is no evidence that he was a mason, the fact that neither he nor Geoffrey was in Staffordshire when the tax of 1332 was collected, suggests that they were engaged on some migratory occupation such as the mason's craft provides.

[1] In a letter from the English Place-Name Society to the present writer, dated 1st October 1943.

[2] William Salt Society, vol. vii, p. 220. See also Addenda p. 68.

Before leaving the subject of "Yevele" as a place-name it should be mentioned that Professor Stenton is able to reject further suggestions relating the name to Northill and Southill on the Bedfordshire river Ivel, and to lands called Iveley in the parish of Hawley near Farnborough, Hants. A supposititious manor of *Yeuele* in Surrey has resulted from faulty indexing of a petition in the Rolls of Parliament (iv, 243a), concerning the possessions of Syon Convent. Other sources show that the reference is to Yeovil, Somerset.

Adopting the identification of Roger de Zeveleye of Uttoxeter with the father of Henry and Robert, it is quite probable that Roger had left Yeaveley in early life, and Henry may perhaps have been born during his father's stay in Uttoxeter. The family cannot have been well off, as Roger paid only 18*d.* to the subsidy, whereas in London in 1332 William de Ramsey, four years before he became the King's Master Mason, was taxed 13*s.* 4*d.* Roger was probably a mason working on such jobs as the building of the towers and spires of Uttoxeter and Ashbourne Churches, then in progress.

Uttoxeter lies only a mile from the Derbyshire border, on an important road leading from Derby and Burton-on-Trent to the Potteries district. Other routes from Lichfield and Stafford to Ashbourne and farther North also pass through the town, and the neighbourhood is rich in the remains of monastic houses. Croxden Abbey, close to the important Hollington freestone quarries, and Rocester Priory, are less than five miles away to the north-west and north, and in the opposite direction lie Tutbury with its Castle and Priory, and Burton-on-Trent whose famous Abbey was the largest monastic house for many miles. Beyond is Repton, the ancient capital of Mercia and seat of a priory, and almost due south is the great cathedral city of Lichfield, the ecclesiastical centre of the region.

The whole district centred politically upon Tutbury, and formed the Honour of Tutbury, a part of the immense Lancaster estates afterwards known as the Duchy of Lancaster. The Honour included parts of Derbyshire, with Yeaveley itself, and stretched southwards almost to Lichfield. The maintenance of Tutbury Castle must have provided periodical work for a number of masons, and such a man as Roger de Yevele may well have secured a permanent position at the Castle or at the neighbouring Priory. If, as is quite likely, Roger worked for Tutbury or some other monastery, Henry and Robert his sons would have had ample opportunities for learning the family craft during childhood and youth, while at the same time attending the monastery school for the normal book-learning of the time. In the fourteenth century an architect of Yevele's importance must have known Court French and Latin as well as English, and his acquaintance with geometry was profound. He learnt, probably from his father, how to draw, to use square and compasses, and to hew freestone, as well as to carve fine detail for tombs and the like, such as those he was to make for his royal patrons in later life. He learnt also the traditions of planning and design (7, 12, 13, 14).

Tomb-carving in particular was a local industry, for around Tutbury were the alabaster quarries which in the later Middle Ages provided material for immense quantities of shop-produced altar-pieces and decorative sculptures.

In the fourteenth century, however, the period of mass production had not been reached, and the few surviving works of this early date are mostly of exquisite quality.

There are few buildings in the neighbourhood which now appear as Henry Yevele knew them in his boyhood, but the splendid Norman nave and west front of Tutbury Priory church are still much as he saw them, and his father

7. SETTING-OUT OF TRACERY: English, c. 1350–1400.
(redrawn) from Pepysian MS. 1916, f.17b.
(Walpole Society, vol. XIII, pl. XVII.)

probably worked on the steeple at Uttoxeter. This was repaired in 1814, but the rest of the church was utterly swept away and rebuilt in 1828. Little remains at Rocester or at Burton Abbey, but there are still extensive remains of the Cistercian Abbey of Croxden, with its severe and noble Early English work. But it is necessary to go farther afield to find the great new works which could have influenced a young architect of the 1330's.

In the Introduction I have briefly sketched the development of the royal school of building, from which it will be seen that during Yevele's boyhood the King's craftsmen at Westminster were creating the Perpendicular style,

8 Westminster Abbey: South and West Walks of Cloister, 1352; 1362

9 Windsor Castle: The Dean's Cloister. 1353
Designer: John Sponlee

11 Wells Cathedral: Retrochoir, looking East, c. 1330
Designer: William Joy

10 Lichfield Cathedral: Presbytery, c. 1337, looking
East to Lady Chapel, c. 1320
Designer of Presbytery: William Ramsey

of which Thomas of Canterbury breathed a suggestion in St. Stephen's Chapel after 1327. Soon afterwards William Ramsey and William Hurley were carrying the new style to Gloucester in the West and Ely in the East, but other ideas tending towards "Perpendicularity" were becoming current, and must now be examined.

The half-century before the Black Death was especially productive of eastern Lady Chapels and lengthened or rebuilt choirs: Lady Chapels were built at Bristol Abbey (c. 1306–32); St. Albans Abbey (c. 1308–26); Reading Abbey (c. 1314–1335); Lichfield Cathedral (c. 1320–30); and Wells Cathedral (c. 1320–26), perhaps also at Evesham Abbey; choirs were lengthened, rebuilt, or remodelled at Bristol Abbey; Winchester Cathedral; Dorchester Abbey, Oxon. (c. 1320–30); Tewkesbury Abbey (c. 1326–49); Wells Cathedral (c. 1329–40); and Gloucester Abbey (1337–49). Great towers were built at Lincoln Cathedral (1306–11); Glastonbury Abbey (early fourteenth century); Wells Cathedral (c. 1320–30); Hereford Cathedral (c. 1325); Pershore Abbey (c. 1330); and Salisbury Cathedral (1334–50), while other important works included the nave of Exeter Cathedral from 1330, the remodelling of the Norman nave of Malmesbury Abbey, the South Transept of Chichester Cathedral (c. 1305–35), and very extensive work at Evesham Abbey, now completely lost. This list includes only the greater works, and does not include the northern Province, which does not seem to have taken part in the formative stage of the Perpendicular style; such works as the nave of York Minster and the magnificent east window of Carlisle Cathedral carried the Curvilinear style to its highest point, and remained unaffected by the changes which were going on in the South.

Several of the important provincial architects are known by name, such as Richard of Stow, the designer of the Lincoln tower, and Richard of Farleigh, who was in charge of the Lady Chapel at Reading and of some work at Bath Abbey in 1334, when he undertook the Salisbury tower; on stylistic grounds, the Pershore tower too must be assigned to him. Thomas Witney was the Exeter architect, being master mason there from 1317 to 1342, and William Joy held a consultant position at Wells for many years after 1319, evidently having other work elsewhere, which may well have included the remodelling of the nave of Malmesbury.

But it was the work at Lichfield which was the most likely to affect the young Henry Yevele, though he probably travelled widely in the ten years which would elapse between the end of his pupilage and the Black Death of 1349. At Lichfield the rebuilding of the cathedral had been in progress for over a century, and by 1320 the work was coming to an end with the completion of the western towers. Attention was transferred to the eastern end of the building and before 1330 a magnificent Lady Chapel had been built some distance to the east of the choir. This chapel is a masterpiece, with a polygonal apse lit by tall three-light windows filled with geometrical tracery. There remained the problem of linking this new chapel to the existing choir. and the chapter decided to seek expert advice from London. On the 23rd of May 1337 they entered into an agreement with Master William of Ramsey,

the King's Master Mason, that he should undertake to advise upon their
works for a fee of £1 for each visit, with 6s. 8d. for the travelling expenses of
himself and his servants coming from London, then a journey of four days
in each direction.

Ramsey's presbytery at Lichfield mingled new features of early Perpendicular character with local details borrowed from the earlier nave, such as the
main wall-ribs carried down without a break inside the piers of the arcades,
and the foliated circles across which these ribs passed. The place of the triforium is taken up with blind tracery whose ribs are a downward continuation
of the window mullions; in all this Ramsey was anticipating the bay-treatment
which was to become normal fifty years later, and which Yevele was to perfect
in his design for the nave of Canterbury Cathedral (10).

From this work at Lichfield Yevele undoubtedly learnt much, but his own
later work shows that he was also influenced by developments farther to the
South and West. From Bristol and Wells he derived the use of a compound
pier, uniting harmoniously the elements of the arch and vault ribs above;
on the other hand, he must have felt the implied poverty of such low vaults as
those of Bristol and Exeter, lovely as they are. Another lesson of the same
sort could be learnt from the nave vault of Tewkesbury, spoilt by crouching
too low over the immense Norman piers. The clear-cut simplicity of the
vaulting in Tewkesbury nave would appeal to Yevele more than the strange
contortions over the choir, or the maze of obscure ribs covering the new
sanctuary of Gloucester. The choir-vault at Pershore, which is probably
Richard of Farleigh's, is a fine example of just those qualities which endeared
themselves to Henry Yevele—sharp definition of pattern against a sufficient
expanse of plain background, with all curves disposed so as to harmonise
with the proportions of the building. The failure of most of the earlier
Gothic architects to achieve a complete unity in design from the floor to
the ridge of the vault is one of the most puzzling problems of art history.
The hard prominence of the diagonal vaulting ribs was often to blame, and
even where this was adjusted, as in the nave of Exeter, there was an imperfect
co-ordination between the parts of the arcade walls. At Salisbury, for
example, the vaulting grows out of the walls almost perfectly, but the bay
design is poor, the main arcade being too high, and the upper stages too
cramped in proportion; the triforium is the worst feature, and is really very
bad indeed. It may be remarked in passing that Salisbury suffers from the
exaggerated eulogies passed on it by the "Early English enthusiasts" of a
couple of generations back: the visitor and the student are led to expect too
much, and the disappointment is correspondingly great. The revulsion of
feeling can even blind one for a time to the great beauty of many of the indi-
vidual parts, the vaults, the triple lancets, and the main arcades. My own
feeling is that the lack of unity at Salisbury is due to imperfect collaboration
between the dilettante Elias de Derham and his master mason Nicholas of
Ely: a collaboration which might be compared with that of the Earl of
Burlington and William Kent.

Like Lichfield, the secular cathedral at Wells had an important influence

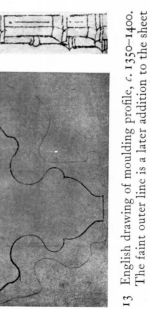

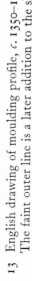

14 Part of a sheet of moulding profiles, English *c.* 1350–1400. The sheet has been cut up to make a sketch-book; the figure bearing sword and flowers is in the dress of *c.* 1485, and is a late palimpsest. The height of the original sketch-book is just under 10 inches.

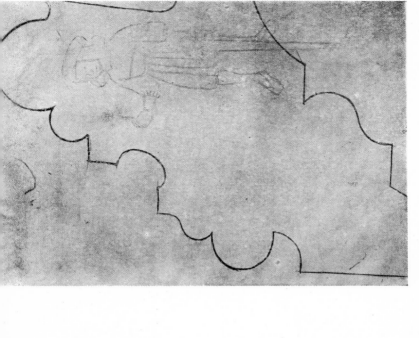

12 English drawing of *c.* 1400

13 English drawing of moulding profile, *c.* 1350–1400. The faint outer line is a later addition to the sheet

16 Wells Cathedral: Central Tower and
Retrochoir. *c.* 1330
Designer: William Joy

15 Worcester Cathedral: Tower from North-west
c. 1365
Designer: John Clyve

on the early Perpendicular medium; by the time Yevele had completed his training, Wells was almost as we know it to-day, except for the western towers; William Joy's new works were being finished by a process of remodelling and the insertion of the remarkable "St. Andrew's arches" to support the new central tower. Joy had become the cathedral architect in time to complete the lovely chapter house, and during the next twenty years carried out a series of most beautiful additions to the fabric. The first of these were the eastern Lady Chapel and the central tower, which latter remarkably anticipates Perpendicular treatment in carrying its vertical divisions straight up through the parapet (16). Other anticipations occur in the retrochoir, where clustered shafts rise the whole height of the bays, carrying the main vaulting ribs; the triforium is occupied by vertical panelling whose divisions rise to a cresting beneath the clerestory windows (11). Perhaps the most interesting feature of all is the great east window, built about 1330, which divides its seven lights into three groups by means of two mullions carried up to the main arch. The tracery of the side divisions employs flowing reticulation and geometrical shapes, while the central tracery has the straight-line reticulations of the new transitional style. It is a pity that the date of this window is not quite certain, as it may well have anticipated William Ramsey's inventions; but even if Ramsey in the course of travel actually saw the work at Wells and adopted its new ideas, the real credit as an inventor must still be awarded to him, for it is clear that William Joy's innovations were accidental; they do not produce the effect of Perpendicular work, whereas Ramsey's do. But the probability is that like many other discoveries, this was made quite independently and simultaneously by two men, each following a similar process of thought and starting from the same premises. The importance of the work at Wells is that it inspired in the later works of Yevele and his colleague William Wynford a strength and solidity which was wanting in the first attempts at Perpendicular made by the royal school of architects.

Church architecture can have been only one of the influences upon Yevele, who also carried out domestic and military works of great importance, but the period of his youth saw far less civil building than was in progress at the great monastic and collegiate churches. The Midland counties are singularly void of domestic remains of this period, and it is now necessary to look elsewhere. For example, there is the fine manor-house at Meare in Somerset, built by Adam Sodbury, Abbot of Glastonbury from 1322 to 1335; he also had building done at some of his other manors. At Meare is a contemporary cottage near the manor, known as the Fish House, in which the Abbey fisherman lived. Both the manor and the fish-house are lit by windows of two lights, with a single reticulation in the head: it was this type of window which Yevele later adapted to Perpendicular forms and used with such success at Westminster Hall (49). It may have been from such simple works as Meare Manor that he acquired his love for plain surfaces of walling, with good buttresses of strong projection.

A little later, in 1341–48, the great manor-house of Penshurst in Kent was built for Sir John de Pulteney, four times mayor of London. Ramsey and

Hurley may have been the architects for this fine house, which includes a hall 64 feet long with a width of 39 feet, roofed in a single span by arch-braced trusses. Penshurst is the first important example of an unaisled domestic hall on a large scale, though a number of halls with spans slightly over 30 feet had been built in castles and monasteries. This grand hall was to be the focal point of the new type of mansion, divorced from military necessities.

Meanwhile, in some parts of the country there was a relapse into less stable conditions, probably due to the opening of the war with France in 1337, and fortifications such as the palace walls and gates at Wells, begun about 1340, and the great gatehouse of Battle Abbey, of the previous year, were the result. Where invasion was to be feared from the directions of France or Scotland, a certain amount of military work was in progress, notably the fine barbican of Lewes Castle in Sussex.

The first cannon were being brought into use, and hand-guns were in England as early as 1338, but the revolutionary effect of gunpowder was not to be fully appreciated for several generations. It was not until after Yevele's death that this necessitated a radically new conception of defence, but it will be seen that his military works included a prophetic realisation of the future; at Queenborough Castle the strictly military fort appeared for the first time, quite divorced from the old type of castle, which had been a fortified residence. But the consideration of Yevele's works must be left to a later chapter, while some attempt is made to sketch the course of events in the last years before the Black Death.

By the time the French War broke out, Yevele was a youth in his pupilage, and he stood on the threshold of his career when the naval battle of Sluys, fought on the 24th of June 1340, secured to Edward III the command of the Channel and cemented his alliance with the Flemings. It led to an uneasy truce which lasted for two years, but from 1342 until 1360 the war became chronic, though interrupted by further truces. The heavy taxation which resulted from the war was probably one of the main causes of the building slump which became quite pronounced after 1340. The withdrawal of men for active service cannot in itself have had much to do with it, for even at the great battle of Crécy in 1346 only about 15,000 English were engaged, apart from Welsh and Irish auxiliaries. The total population is not likely to have been more than about five millions, inclusive of Wales.

Certainly the period must have put considerable difficulties in the way of an ambitious young architect, and the main road to success was the "royal" road of entering the King's service. In spite of the war, the King was spending great sums of money at Westminster and Windsor Castle. In the three years 1344–46, Edward III resumed the practice of impressment on a large scale to recruit masons for Windsor Castle, and also for the works at Corfe Castle and Westminster. It is very likely that Henry Yevele and his brother Robert were thus impressed, or else that they sought employment at one of these buildings on their own account. Less probably, they may have found their time fully occupied on private building works, or perhaps on works on the Lancaster estates, and have entered the King's service only after the Black Death, when the demand for brilliant young men had enormously increased. Until further records of their movements come to light, it is idle to speculate concerning the details of their careers, but Henry must have carried out a good deal of work by the time he appears as one of the chief London masons in 1356, by which time he was in his middle thirties.

The non-fighting men of the Middle Ages were nearly as long-lived as in more modern times, though periods of pestilence and famine must have brought down the average age at death. The tendency of the period was, however, towards precocity, and the degree of independence reached at twenty-one in the fourteenth century is now seldom realised before thirty. Thus by the time Yevele was thirty-five, he would already have had long experience behind him and have possessed the self-reliance which in modern times is associated with later middle life. Certainly he must have designed houses and probably church and military works as well, besides acquiring interests as a contractor and a stone-merchant; doubtless also as an alabaster carver in Derbyshire, where he could have learnt the specialised knowledge of tomb design which he displayed so often in the latter part of his career. Much later he had interests in the Isle of Purbeck, and translated the alabaster details into the terms of the stronger and coarser-grained marble.

Alternatively, Yevele may have gone with the English armies into France and have seen something of the great French churches, tall and graceful, yet somewhat antiquated to an English eye. France was suffering from the war in a way that England never experienced; whole districts were ravaged by the march and countermarch of armies, and still worse, were looted by the free companies of mercenaries. Under such circumstances the expenditure of large sums on immovables was impossible, and the fourteenth century in France produced very little architecture, though the other arts were in full bloom. Guillaume de Machaut, the greatest poet north of the Alps, was also the principal composer of his time, writing ballades, motets and masses, and remarkable instrumental works in several parts. Born about 1300 in Champagne, he spent thirty years in the service of John, King of Bohemia, with whom he travelled across Europe as far as Russia, and after King John's death at Crécy, settled in Normandy, obtaining a Court appointment from King John of France in 1350. France was also linked to the southern world of literature by Giovanni Boccaccio, whose mother was a Parisian, while he himself visited France. New ideas in painting were also spreading from Italy, where the great Giotto had died in 1337, and somewhere in France was born André Beauneveu, who was to be the greatest northern portraitist of the next fifty years.

Influences from central and southern Europe reached England by various routes, even through France, for the war did not prevent courtly intercourse between the cultured leaders on both sides. The King of England was himself a great international figure, as his pedigree and diplomatic history show. Grandson of Edward I and Eleanor, daughter of St. Ferdinand, King of Castile, his other grandparents were Philip the Fair, King of France, and Joan, daughter of King Henry of Navarre; his Queen, Philippa of Hainault, was closely related to the Houses of Luxembourg, Valois, and Anjou-Sicily. The Flemings, linked to England by the wool trade, recognised Edward's claim to be King of France and thus their suzerain, with the result that his court was often held in the Low Countries, which formed an important base for his expeditions into France.

It must not be thought that England was lacking in important artists and men of letters and science. The painter Hugh of St. Albans was producing lovely mural decorations at St. Stephen's and in the Chapter House at Westminster, and was in touch with artistic developments in Italy, for when he died in 1368 he left a painting of Lombardy, comprising seven pieces, which had cost him £20. In 1361 died the great physician Dr. John Gaddesden, who had produced a treatise which was to enjoy an European reputation for centuries; of far more modern outlook was his junior colleague John Ardern of Newark, one of the fathers of modern surgery, and author of an important work in which he clearly and most modestly expounded the results of his long experience during the French war and elsewhere.

The older religious school of literature had culminated in the famous mystic Richard Rolle, who died in 1349; by that date a vintner's son in London was nine years old and beginning to make mental notes of all that went on around him: his name was Geoffrey Chaucer. The future diplomat and secret service man would also in the fullness of time be chief of the office of works for two years, and in close contact with Henry Yevele, but all his hardworking official career was later to be eclipsed by the importance of his literary labours.

Chaucer, unlike de Machaut, did not add musical composition to his poetic gifts, and music in England lagged behind the other arts; when Edward III on his ship the "Cog Thomas" was awaiting the attack of the Spanish fleet off Winchelsea in 1350, Froissart relates that "he ordered his minstrels to play before him a German dance which Sir John Chandos had lately introduced. For his amusement he made the same knight sing with his minstrels, which delighted him greatly." It was not until the last quarter of the century that an important English school of counterpoint began to find its feet, perhaps under the leadership of King Richard II, whose compositions are unfortunately lost; about the same time, c. 1380, was born John Dunstable. Dunstable, the greatest composer Europe had known, was the musical counterpart of Chaucer and Yevele, though he was only starting his career when they died. He sprang, however, from the same great cultural epoch, and his death in 1453 marked its close, coinciding with the expulsion of the English from France, and the fall of Constantinople.

This was the new world which was ready to blossom forth at the time when Henry Yevele was seeking his first commissions and taking his earliest contracts. The victory of Crécy was one of the most astonishing successes in military history, and if the world were in fact ruled by military success, Edward III would have been the master of Europe, and England the richest country in the West. Edward did in fact succeed in founding an order of knighthood which made Windsor the centre of chivalry, and in 1348 he was offered the crown of the Empire. This he refused, probably on account of his financial difficulties. War, even victorious war, is not the highroad to prosperity, and though Edward's success was not limited to Crécy, but included also the taking of Calais and of David, King of Scots, yet there was no decision, and no sign of any end to the constant drain on the national resources.

At this moment occurred the greatest calamity in the history of Europe: Asiatic Plague was introduced from Tartary by way of Genoese ships trading to the Crimea, and via the Levant and North Africa to Sicily and Greece. By the end of 1347 the disease had reached Provence and in a few months spread over all France, practically depopulated the Channel Islands, and was brought thence into Dorset. By November 1348 it had reached London, though the worst was to come in the next summer, when 50,000 died in the capital alone. London suffered more than the country districts, but the population as a whole was reduced in two years to half or one-third of its level in 1347, leaving perhaps little over two millions, where they may have been five before. The continent was for the most part less affected than England, but everywhere there must have been a terrible dislocation of trade and normal life. Edward III has been much criticised for continuing the court revels and pageants on as grand a scale as ever, but this is hardly fair: the apparently insane gaiety of the royal household was only natural under the circumstances, and it served to ensure the continuance of the cultural traditions which would otherwise have perished.

Many died, perhaps more than half England, but still many lived, and among the survivors was Henry Yevele. Since the mortality among the London craftsmen was very high indeed, his escape suggests that he was still working in the provinces, or else that he was able to leave the capital. No sooner was the worst of the epidemic over than the King had the works re-started at Windsor and Westminster, and the demand for skilled craftsmen and designers greatly exceeded the supply. The King's mason William Ramsey had died in the plague, and so had his brother John; new men were brought in to fill their places, John atte Grene from Ely Minster, and John Box from Canterbury Cathedral, while John Sponlee, possibly from Winchcombe Abbey, was put in charge at Windsor Castle.

If Yevele had not settled in London before this, he must have done so now, for he can hardly have been a newcomer in 1356, when he was one of the principal freestone masons of the city. The devastated metropolis must have been a gloomy enough place, but houses would have been cheap to those who cared to take the risk, and Yevele and his brother Robert were of stout heart. The wave of religious feeling which proclaimed that the visitation was the Hand of God naturally led to a spate of "good works," including the provision of tombs and chantry chapels for the more distinguished victims. Here was the chance for which Henry had waited and worked; probably in partnership with his brother Robert, behold him established in London as designer and carver of tombs and monuments, prepared to undertake also such nobler work as should offer.

Chapter II
Success

THE AMOUNT OF NEW BUILDING WORK IN LONDON WHICH WAS begun just after the plague is surprising, and included extensive works at four great churches. The largest of these was a new foundation, the Cistercian Abbey of St. Mary Eastminster, whose site is now covered by the Royal Mint. This house was founded in 1350 by the King himself, and the whole work was completed under royal auspices. Unfortunately, the monastery was "clean pulled down" shortly after its surrender in 1539, as Stow records. Queen Philippa, in 1351, founded a chantry in the nearby hospital of St. Katharine's, and Hollar's engraving of the church shows aisles which appear to be of about this date, as well as a western porch much resembling the type afterwards employed by Yevele. The aisle windows are of three lights, with straight reticulations in the heads, while the mullions are carried down below the sill to form the "long-panel" design used by William Ramsey for the chapter-house at St. Paul's.

The aisles at St. Katharine's were, however, quite clearly Perpendicular, and were much plainer than Ramsey's chapter-house. The work may well have been done by Yevele, and would have brought him into contact with the royal establishment, as the hospital was close by the Tower of London, as well as the growing Abbey of Eastminster. In addition to these works for royal patrons, two of London's friary churches were being rebuilt by great noblemen: Hugh Courtenay earl of Devonshire began extensive works at the Whitefriars, in the western suburb of London, and Humfrey Bohun earl of Hereford and Essex re-edified the church of the Austin Friars in 1354. Little beyond the plan of Whitefriars is known, but the nave of Austin Friars survived the dissolution and the Great Fire, to show that it was conceived in a backward style. The clerestory was omitted, while the large aisle windows were of pure Decorated character, of the best Curvilinear type, the great west window being Geometric. The new style, though uniformly employed in works under royal patronage, was not yet firmly established as the prevailing fashion.

At this time the London masons had no regular gild or fraternity to administer their craft, and disputes arose between the hewers on the one hand, and the layers and setters on the other. The hewers tended to form the aristocracy of the trade, and among the hewers were to be found those master masons in freestone who were the principal architects of the period, being skilled not merely in the actual cutting of stone, but in the traditions of planning and design. Evidently the main subject at issue was the usage of hewers to work as setters on occasion, or *vice versa*, and the quarrel became so grave that the Mayor and Aldermen had to interfere. The mayor of 1355–56 was Simon Francis or Fraunceys, a mercer, and on the 1st of February 1355–6 he presided over a congregation held at the Guildhall to ordain articles for the trade of masons, with a view to remedying the dissensions.

The "good folks of the trade" had chosen from among themselves twelve of their most skilful men, of whom six represented the hewers, and the other six the layers and setters. They were sworn before the Mayor and Aldermen to inform them "as to the acts and articles touching their said trade," and the eight articles propounded by the twelve masons were ordered to be observed under pain of fines to the use of the Commonalty of London. The six masons elected by the hewers were Walter and Richard de Sallynge, Thomas de Bredone, John de Tyryngtone, Thomas de Gloucestre, and Henry de Yeevelee. The two Sallynges were probably sons of an earlier Walter de Salynge, mason, who had died in 1339; Richard had worked at Windsor in 1350–51 and was warden of the King's masons at Hadleigh Castle in 1362–64, while in 1363 he was sworn as one of the surveyors of his craft in the city. Nothing is known of the career of Bredone, but Tyryngton worked for the Black Prince at Kennington in 1351, and Thomas of Gloucester had been warden of the masons at the Tower of London since 1354, being paid at the rate of 6*d.* a day. About the time these regulations were made, he was transferred to Westminster, where he was the chief mason working on St. Stephen's Chapel, and warden there until 1359. Gloucester was one of the most important masons in the King's service, and Yevele may also have been employed on the royal works.

The articles approved were briefly: that every man of the trade, if he were perfectly skilled, might do any type of work; that "good folks of the trade" should be chosen and sworn when needful, to see that no mason took work which he was not skilful enough to complete; that no one should undertake contract work without bringing at least four "ancient men of the trade," prepared to testify to his ability and to guarantee completion if he should fail; that no one should set an apprentice or journeyman to work except in the presence of his master; no apprentice to be taken for a less term than seven years; the sworn Masters to see that day-workers were paid according to their deserts "and not outrageously"; that any one of the trade refusing to obey the sworn Masters should be reported to the Mayor, who would have power by assent of the Aldermen and Sheriffs, to punish him by imprisonment and otherwise; and that no one should take the journeyman or apprentice of another to his master's prejudice, until his term should have fully expired.

Yevele, at the age of about thirty-five, was thus ranked as one of the "most skilful men" of his trade, in association with masons of old standing in the city, and with one of the principal masons in the King's service. If he was already living in the neighbourhood of London Bridge, his next step towards success can be easily explained. At the upper end of Fish Street Hill, only a hundred yards or so from Yevele's parish church of St. Magnus, there was, to quote Stow who saw it, "one great house, for the most part built of stone, which pertained sometime to Edward the Black Prince, . . . who was in his lifetime lodged there." Two centuries later it had become "a common hostelry, having the Black Bell for a sign," but in 1357 it reached the pinnacle of its glory, when the prince rode through the city with his captive, King John the Good of France. The prince's great victory at Poitiers on the 19th of September 1356 had made him an European hero, and the next few years were the most splendid in his career.

Prince Edward's chief residence near London was the manor of Kennington in Surrey, some two miles south of London Bridge along the Roman Stane Street. For more than two years the prince remained in England, and one of his first cares was the refitting of Kennington Palace. Before the Black Death the prince's master mason had been Nicholas Ailyngton, but he had probably died of the plague, and works carried out in 1351 and later had been done by the masons John Tyryngton and John Pouke. Tyryngton and Pouke apparently died, leaving the work unfinished, about 1357, and it is probable that the prince, when at his city house, heard of the rising mason who lived down the street, and after seeing some of his work decided to give him a trial. At any rate, in March 1358 Henry Yevele undertook a contract whereby he was to build certain walls, chimneys and staircases at Kennington, for which the prince would pay £221 4s. 7d.; this work had been completed and the money paid by September 1359, but by this time Yevele held a post as the prince's mason, by which title he was referred to when the prince ordered his receiver-general to pay Yevele £60, on the 25th of October 1359. The prince was then leaving the country with Edward III, who had undertaken a new invasion of France; though not as successful as he had hoped, it led to the conclusion of peace on very advantageous terms, at Brétigny near Chartres on the 8th of May 1360.

The peace of Brétigny was the last of the great successes of the reign, but at the time it seemed that victory had put an end to the unhappy years which had begun with the plague in 1348. The King could at last push forward with the immense works at Windsor Castle, which had been delayed during the years of pestilence and campaigning. Other work was needed at the palaces, manors and castles which maintained his royal state throughout the country, and men of talent were needed to take the place of the "stop-gaps" who had been appointed after the plague casualties. John atte Grene was dead, and John Sponlee at Windsor was getting old. The hour had come, and Henry Yevele received a grant of the office of "disposer of the King's works pertaining to the art of masonry in the Palace of Westminster and the Tower of London," with fees of 12d. a day. These fees, payable for 365 days in the year, were equivalent to some £500 a year in modern values, and the position was in effect that of Chief Architect for the whole of southern England. Yevele for the first nine years held the office "at the King's pleasure," not for life, but even so he could feel confident that he had arrived at a considerable degree of success. He was about forty, and in the full enjoyment of his powers, which were to increase as time went on.

He had probably married by now, but all that is known of Margaret his first wife is that her sister Isabella was married to William Palmer, a citizen and horse-dealer of London, a fact which does at least suggest that Yevele's marriage was in London and to a Londoner.[1]

It is likely that this was not Yevele's first experience of the royal service, but even so there would have been much to learn on becoming the principal technical officer of this great department. In 1360 the head of the administration was William of Lambeth, clerk and surveyor of the works, who had held office for some four years; next to him in importance was the comptroller who took his name from the counter-roll of expenditure which it was his duty to keep, and from which the accounts prepared by the clerk and surveyor were audited. A generation or two later the grants of office to these appointments contain a certain amount of detail, which probably applies to Yevele's day and even earlier. The clerk and surveyor had a dwelling-house and "long garden" on the west side of Westminster Hall, with a small counting-house and several storehouses, one of them known as "Hell," in the vaults beneath the Long House of the Exchequer, which jutted out westwards from the north end of the hall. The clerk's house served for "the adminstration and preservation of the books" and for "the attendance and resort of the people and officers" in connection with the works. There were also chambers called "traceris" or tracing-houses, where the working drawings were made, and in the counting-houses worked the engrossing clerks to the clerk and the controller, making up the long rolls of particulars of income and expenditure, of which many are still in existence. Besides the clerical officers and the chief mason and carpenter, the King's glazier was housed close by, having control of the "shedde called the Glasiers Logge," which was 60 feet long and 20 broad.

At the Tower of London other officers lived and worked in houses on the wharf: the purveyor, whose duty it was to obtain materials and sometimes labour, the chief smith, the serjeant plumber, and the chief joiner. Both the Tower and Westminster Palace were on the bank of the Thames, the great highway of old London, and there was always much coming and going between the two places. Unlike the grimy remains known to the modern tourist, the mediaeval castle and palace were bright places gaily coloured and set with gardens; the keep of the Tower is still known as the White Tower from the ancient habit of giving it a coat of whitewash from time to time to keep the grime at bay, for even in the thirteenth and fourteenth centuries London had a growing smoke nuisance. (Frontispiece)

When Yevele took charge of this great establishment, the Controller was Adam of Chesterfield, one of the King's clerks, and the purveyor was John of Alkeshull; these were posts usually held for comparatively short terms, as a form of preferment, but the chief craftsmen, who held office for long terms of years, were the men who influenced and formed the style of the time.

[1] See pedigree at end of book.

Next to that of master mason, the office of chief carpenter was the most important, and had been held by William Herland since Hurley's death in 1354. He had been Hurley's chief assistant at Windsor and at St. Stephen's Chapel, and after his death designed the roof of the new Windsor great hall, besides working on the stalls of St. Stephen's. In 1358 he had been put in charge of repairs at Hadleigh Castle in Essex, near Leigh-on-Sea, and spent a year or so there, but by the summer of 1360 he was back at Westminster with his son Hugh as his chief assistant. Carpentry was in their blood, for Master John Herland had been in charge of the timberwork at Westminster in 1329, and one Michael Herland, who died about 1390, was another London carpenter. Hugh, the most important member of the family, was destined to work in close collaboration with Yevele in after years.

John Geddyng seems to have been the chief glazier at this time, but not much is known about his career, and on the important glazing at St. Stephen's a large number of glaziers had been employed. The chief smith at the Tower was Andrew "le Fevre" who had succeeded his father Walter "of Bury" in 1345; he evidently inherited smithing from both sides of his ancestry, for when in 1346 he went to France in the King's train, to serve at Crécy, his widowed mother Katharine was granted the wages of the office, 8d. a day, on condition of keeping up "the King's forge within the Tower" and carrying on its work. The smith's work was very varied, for he had to provide iron-work of all descriptions, from arms to decorative grilles, hinges, and other "furniture"; in 1357 he had made ironwork for the chamber of the captive King of France, while two years later he supplied 65 great nails for the lions' house in the Tower, three of the nails weighing over a pound. Since the "piece of ironwork" for the King of France's room weighed 210 pounds, and was provided "by order of the Treasurer," it is to be feared that the chivalrous treatment of the royal prisoner did not extend as far as trusting him not to escape, and it may be that the memory of this very *ferramentum* provoked the noble remark made by him on a later occasion. After the peace of Brétigny he was allowed to return to France, leaving his son Louis of Anjou as a hostage in Calais while he attempted to raise his ransom. The young prince escaped in 1363, whereupon King John gave himself up to the English to redeem his honour, saying: "*Si la bonne foi était bannie du reste de la terre, elle devrait se retrouver dans le coeur et dans la bouche des rois.*" (If good faith were to disappear from the rest of the earth, it should still be found in the hearts and mouths of kings.)

Besides the regular works "establishment," Westminster Palace saw a great deal of the old painter Hugh of St. Albans, whose lovely figures of angels in St. Stephen's Chapel were attracting so much attention. Another frequenter of the palace was young Geoffrey Chaucer, just released from his imprisonment in France, and now attached to the Court. He had probably managed to bring back with him a copy of the famous *Roman de la Rose* which he was beginning to translate into English verse. Besides forming a rendezvous for men of art and letters, the Court at Westminster formed the centre of the legal life of the country, and learned men and students from all

17 Canterbury Cathedral: Black Prince's Chantry, *c.* 1363

18 Canterbury Cathedral: Tomb of the Black Prince, 1376

19 Westminster Abbey: Gatehouse over Outer Parlour and
Cloister Entry, from West. 1362

20 Westminster Abbey: Abbot's Hall from South-east, 1372.
An example of Yevele's mastery of wall surfaces and fenestration

parts of England and the Continent were constantly to be found in the great hall or at the abbey close by.

From the steady trade of a city craftsman Yevele found himself transported to this whirling centre of life, and in charge of the buildings in which the King and courtiers had their being. Not only this, but he had also to devise new buildings for a King who was one of the greatest patrons of architecture in English history. His tenure of office was marked by an immediate activity, and on the 13th of August he was authorised to impress masons and set them to work at the King's wages for as long as was necessary, and to commit them to prison if they refused such work; three days later a similar commission was granted to William and Hugh Herland, the carpenters.

The works in question were at Westminster and the Tower, and the actual supervision of the work was deputed to the masons' warden, Thomas of Gloucester, whose business it was to "ordain the work" of the men during the absence of the master. The post of warden was one of considerable responsibility, for he had to be "trewe mene bitwene his master & his felaws and . . . besy (busy) in the absence of his master to the honor of his master and profit to the lorde tht he serveth," as the "Points of Masonry" declare.

At the Tower, Yevele's brother Robert was able to secure an important contract for £55 worth of work, something like a £1500 job now, and in 1362 became warden of the masons there. No doubt he owed his good fortune largely to family influence, but there are influences far worse than nepotism, and the vault beneath the Bloody Tower with its lions' heads for corbels and lions' faces for bosses, still stands to show that Robert earned his money well.

The year 1361, which saw Robert building this vault and other works at the Tower, found Henry designing another castle of an entirely new type. This was the famous fort for coastal defence, built at Queenborough in Kent on the Isle of Sheppey. The town was named by Edward III in honour of Queen Philippa, and made a free borough under a mayor and two bailiffs, while the port was of considerable importance. The flat land by the mouth of the Medway offered no temptations as a royal residence, with the result that the castle could be designed purely as a garrison fortress, without state apartments, and planned entirely for military purposes (21, 22).

Yevele's plan was a triumph of clear thinking and simplicity: the whole fort was contained within a circular wall, whose radius was 10 perches or 165 feet, and which was surrounded by a moat. The entrance was on the west, and consisted of a normal gateway between two round towers, while on the east side, exactly opposite, there was a postern. Concentric with the outer curtain was a higher range of buildings, also circular on plan, with a radius of 4 perches, or 66 feet; around this were placed six semicircular towers, continuing high above the inner curtain wall, the two eastern towers being brought together to guard the entrance to the inner ward. An enemy penetrating the outer gate would still have to pass half-way round the inner ward exposed to heavy fire from above, before attacking the inner gate which led to the whole of the habitable chambers, disposed around the small circular court in the centre. The great well was sunk at the central point of the plan. The high inner curtain, as was normal in the earlier concentric castles, commanded the low outer wall, so that archers on both could fire at once upon an enemy

21. QUEENBOROUGH CASTLE: View from North-west,
after a drawing by Hollar. 1361.

without. The power of early cannon had not yet become great enough to be taken into account, so that the high walls and inner circle of towers were still a sound solution of the problem. As it happened, Queenborough was

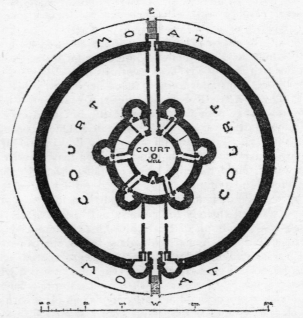

22. QUEENBOROUGH CASTLE: Ground Plan. 1361. Traced from a drawing in the Hatfield MSS. by A. W. Clapham.

never put to the proof, and was demolished by the Parliament in 1650, but it provided a model for the much later circular forts of Henry VIII, which were modified to suit the changed conditions of warfare.

Here, at the outset of his official career, Yevele showed himself far in advance of his time, and acquired a reputation for military architecture which brought him a great deal of work on fortifications in later years. Furthermore, the clerk of works in charge of the building was William of Wykeham, who had been transferred from Windsor Castle, and who on the conclusion of the work at Queenborough was given the Bishopric of Winchester, and became one of the leading figures in the country. Yevele's acquaintance with Wykeham lasted until the end of his life, and the two great men must have been of service to each other in many ways.

During these years Yevele was normally stationed at "headquarters," where considerable work was in progress. The actual supervision of the work at Queenborough was put into the hands of Master John Box, the Canterbury mason who had joined the King's service in 1350. The accounts for 1362 name Yevele "deviser of masonry" to the King, a term equivalent to the modern use of the word "architect," which for some unexplained reason was seldom used in mediaeval times. In the previous October his old patron the Black Prince had married his cousin Joan, "the Fair Maid of Kent," who was countess of Kent in her own right, and widow of Sir Thomas Holland. In order to marry, the cousins had to obtain a papal dispensation on account of their consanguinity, and as a condition agreed to found a chantry in Canterbury Cathedral. In 1362 the prince was granted the French dominions of the Crown, with the title of Prince of Aquitaine, and with his wife left England early in the following year for Bordeaux, where they kept a brilliant court for the following eight years. Before leaving he made arrangements that part of the crypt at Canterbury should be transformed into a chantry chapel where the agreed masses might be sung (17).

The crypt in question lay beneath the south-eastern transept of the cathedral, and was entirely remodelled, being provided with clustered shafts and lierne vaulting, as well as new windows. There can be little doubt that this work was to Yevele's design, though he must have arranged with some other mason, perhaps John Box, to undertake the necessary supervision. Canterbury, however, possessed a royal castle, and so did Dover, and Yevele must have had official business from time to time which would take him through the Kentish capital.

About the same time, that is to say beginning in 1362, the Abbot of Westminster, Nicholas Litlyngton, set about the building of a new house for himself to the west of the Abbey cloister (19, 20). The south and west cloisters were not completed until 1365, having taken about thirteen years to build, under John Palterton, the Abbey's master mason. There are strong reasons for thinking that Palterton was not the architect, or that he was acting in a subordinate capacity, and if so the real designer can only have been Yevele. It was pointed out by Lethaby that the plan of the new nave and western towers must have been set out before the west cloisters and the Abbot's House were built. It is generally agreed that the scheme of rebuilding the Norman nave originated with Langham, who was Abbot from 1349 to 1362, but that no actual work was carried out until after 1375. It is none the less plain from an examination of the structure, that Lethaby was right, and the date of setting-out for the whole of the new work is thus carried back to 1362 at the latest. There can be no doubt as to Yevele's responsibility for the new work of the nave from the 1370's, and he was certainly working for the Abbey as early as 1372 so that it seems reasonable to suppose that he was called in by Langham about the time of his Crown appointment in 1360. There is also evidence from the other side which clinches this argument: the Infirmary buildings were rebuilt between 1364 and 1372, and the accounts make it plain that John Palterton was directly responsible for the work, which included a carved doorway to the little Cloister, still in existence. This doorway was built in 1371–72, but its details are much earlier, more Decorated in character, than the west cloister, which was certainly finished in 1365. Here is definite structural evidence for the employment of two designers at the same time, and shows that Yevele was a "progressive" in comparison to the conservative Palterton, who was by no means of the same high standing, his fees amounting only to 2s. a week, with a daily allowance of bread and beer, and a yearly sum of £2.

I have gone into some detail on this point, because the west cloister is an important early Perpendicular work, and the Abbot's House one of the finest mediaeval houses left, and the only one of comparable interest anywhere near London. Fortunately, it can be dated with accuracy, and it is even possible to give some details of its progress. The Jerusalem Chamber was sufficiently far advanced by 1372 to have its windows temporarily filled with canvas, and the hall followed, the glazing being done by 1376. The hall has a beautiful timber roof, designed by one of the Herlands, and the window tracery is much like that of the west cloister, combining Geometric and Perpendicular motives in a fresh and charming way. Two beautiful windows of Yevele's design have lately been revealed by the destruction of the more recent buildings of the Deanery. The tracery is perfect and original, though blocked, and formerly lit the now dark passage leading from the south-west corner of the great Cloister into Dean's Yard.

Although Yevele had come to Court, he had not deserted the City, and in 1365 appears as one of the two Wardens of London Bridge. The Wardens were administrative officials elected by the Mayor, Aldermen and Common Council on the 21st of September each year. They held office from Michaelmas to Michaelmas, each warden receiving a fee of £10 for his services. The duties involved great responsibility, as the City held in trust large estates from whose revenue the Bridge had to be maintained. These estates included the Stocks Market, and the market and leasehold houses as well as the Bridge itself, required constant maintenance. Besides responsibility for the work, the wardens had to prepare accounts of revenue and expenditure for audit, and to look after the large staff of workmen employed. On the Bridge itself was their headquarters, the Bridge House, and beside the house stood the Chapel of St. Thomas, built upon a great pier and consisting of a crypt and an upper chapel (Frontispiece).

Yevele was annually re-elected as one of the Wardens for many years,

23 Westminster Palace: North Front of Great Hall. 1394

24 Westminster Palace: Clock Tower. 1365
From an engraving after Hollar

25 Shene Palace: on right, ruined Hall of old Palace, shortly before demolition, 1562

and may have held the post continuously until 1395, after which he was compelled by age to relinquish its duties. The fee of £10 yearly, amounting to quite £250 in our values, made a very substantial difference to his income, and he was also able to augment it by his private business in building materials.

It seems strange to modern ideas that a prominent architect and civil servant should then himself have sold materials for use in Crown works, but in spite of more rigid class distinctions, there was little artificial snobbery in the fourteenth century. Particularly in the City of London it was quite normal for men of mercantile families to rise in social status until they could mix almost on equal terms with the armorial gentry. Chaucer was son of a vintner, and in 1363 another vintner, Henry Picard, had feasted four Kings at his house on the same day, and Stow relates that they were "Edward III King of England, John King of France, David King of Scots, the King of Cyprus, then all in England," and adds that there were also present "Edward prince of Wales, with many other noblemen, and after (Picard) kept his hall for all comers that were willing to play at dice and hazard." Consequently it is not particularly surprising that Henry Yevele, while "Director of the Works" at Westminster Palace in 1365, was also paid for 7000 Flanders tiles for paving the Palace courtyards, and for a quantity of plaster of Paris. In that and the following year he seems to have been stationed at headquarters during the building of the great clock-tower on the north side of the court in front of Westminster Hall (24).

As in so many other cases, accurate knowledge of the tower depends on Hollar's views which show that it rose high above the houses, comprising (above the roof level) a blind storey with the clock on its southern face, and above a belfry stage lit by three-light windows with traceried heads. By the seventeenth century the tower was crowned with a plain parapet and low pyramidal roof, though this may not have been the original finish. The tower was famous for its clock, and for the great bell on which the hours were struck, the strokes being heard as far as the city. Architecturally the tower had no pretensions beyond its fine proportions and simplicity, which are paralleled in the town belfry at St. Albans. The St. Albans clock-tower was probably built early in the fifteenth century, and may well have been designed by Thomas Wolvey, a prominent St. Albans mason who, as will be seen, worked under Yevele at Westminster Hall shortly before 1400.

By this time the work at Queenborough Castle was drawing to a close, and so was the immense rebuilding scheme at Windsor Castle, where William Wynford had become joint architect with John Sponlee. Wynford's career will be considered later, but it may be remarked that he was a Somerset man and apparently a few years younger than Yevele, though their careers were roughly contemporary. The great works of Edward III were practically finished, and for the last ten years of the reign building activity at Court became of less importance. There was still plenty of maintenance work going on, and in 1368 Yevele was supplying freestone from Stapleton in Yorkshire for the repair of Rochester Castle; next year the French War was renewed, owing to the repudiation by Charles V of France of the terms settled at Brétigny.

This year, 1369, was the beginning of the gloomy close to Edward III's glorious reign of half a century; Queen Philippa lay ill at Windsor and died on the 14th of August, sincerely lamented for her generosity and kind and merciful disposition. The King's craftsmen had cause to remember the good queen, for at the great tournament held in Cheapside in 1331 "there was a wooden scaffold erected across the street, like unto a tower, wherein Queen Philippa, and many other ladies, richly attired, and assembled from all parts of the realm, did stand to behold the jousts; but the higher frame, in which the ladies were placed, brake in sunder, whereby they were with some shame forced to fall down, by reason whereof the knights, and such as were underneath, were grievously hurt; wherefore the queen took great care to save the carpenters from punishment, and through her prayers (which she made upon her knees) pacified the king and council, and thereby purchased great love of the people."

Within a fortnight of her death, on the 27th of August, Yevele received a new grant of his office under improved conditions: he was to hold it for life, instead of "during pleasure," and was to have a winter robe of the suit of the Esquires of the Household. He was thus put upon a footing with men of much higher birth, and at the queen's funeral a few days later took his place among the minor esquires of the Court, with William Wynford. Both masons were given a special issue of black cloth for their mourning apparel.

Through this summer the third pestilence had been raging (the second had been in 1361–62), and among the victims was the young Duchess Blanche of Lancaster, wife of John of Gaunt, who was absent in France at the head of an invading army. The duke's absence delayed the preparation of his wife's tomb in St. Paul's Cathedral, but on his return the work was in 1374 entrusted to Yevele, who took into partnership Thomas Wreck, a London mason-contractor. The tomb and its great carved canopy were destroyed in the Great Fire, but Hollar's engravings show a splendid monument, and the price was correspondingly high, amounting to £486, well over £10,000 of our money (51). While Yevele was engaged on the Duchess's tomb, Chaucer was writing the Book of the Duchesse as a tribute to her memory.

The renewed invasion of France led to the pressing of masons for foreign service, and Yevele was commissioned in 1370 to take such men and bring them to Orwell Haven in Suffolk, then one of the great ports. In this year work began on the College of chantry priests founded by John Lord Cobham at Cobham in Kent, while a simple western tower and richly carved sedilia were added to Cobham Church. In view of Yevele's later works for Lord Cobham, it is exceedingly likely, as Mr. Christopher Hussey suggests,[1] that he was the designer. Cobham College seems to have been the earliest example of that type of quadrangular college plan wherein separate dwelling places are provided, analogous to the cells of Carthusian monasteries.[2] It is perhaps more than a remarkable coincidence that Yevele in the following year, 1371, besides impressing masons for overseas service of the Crown, secured the

---

[1] Country Life, 4 and 11 February, 1944.
[2] cf. W. H. Godfrey in Some Famous Buildings, pp. 220, 225.

27 Canterbury: West Gate from within. 1378

26 Canterbury: West Gate from without. 1378

28 Westminster Abbey: Tomb of Edward III, from the
South-west. 1377

important £600 contract for building the first section of the London Charter-house (29).

This priory was founded by Sir Walter Manny, the famous Flemish knight in Edward III's service. At the time of the great plague of 1349, Sir Walter had purchased thirteen acres of ground from St. Bartholomew's hospital, and had it consecrated as a burial place for the victims. After the third great plague, he arranged for the building of a house of Carthusian monks beside the cemetery, and obtained Yevele's services as architect and contractor for the first cell and a section of the great cloister; presumably the whole of the original planning and design was also Yevele's. Since there were only some

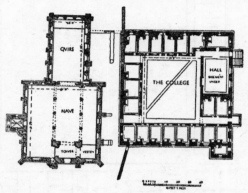

29. COBHAM CHURCH AND COLLEGE: Ground Plan. 1370.

half-dozen Charterhouses in England at the time, Yevele's task was a novel one, for the Carthusian monasteries were on an entirely different plan from those of the other orders. Instead of living a communal life, each monk lived in seclusion in his own cell and had his own garden, the cells being spaced round a large cloister, which at London was nearly 300 feet square, provision being made for a community of twenty-four monks, including their prior (30). In addition to the buildings, Yevele probably designed the founder's tomb, of which a lovely fragment remains (31).

Yevele's ability to take on such large private contracts suggests that his official duties were comparatively slight at this period, which is what would be expected from the cessation of all large royal building works. While still engaged on the Charterhouse he undertook to build the bridge between Chelmsford and Moulsham in Essex, which was maintained at the expense of Westminster Abbey. In 1372 he received a sum of £23 6s. 8d. for this work, and he was probably working for Abbot Litlyngton at the Abbey as well. He may have been able to combine visits to Chelmsford with journeys on official business, for he had at the same time to search for masons who could be impressed for service in London and Sandwich—the latter presumably for the futile expedition which the King tried to lead into France, but which was unable to land owing to contrary winds. The state of affairs in France was rapidly becoming worse, for ill-health had compelled the Black Prince to return to England, and John of Gaunt was quite unable to stem the tide of French reaction.

For three years Yevele almost disappears from view, owing to the stoppage of all royal work of importance; he must have been engaged on the Abbot's House at Westminster, but otherwise he seems to have profited by his leisure

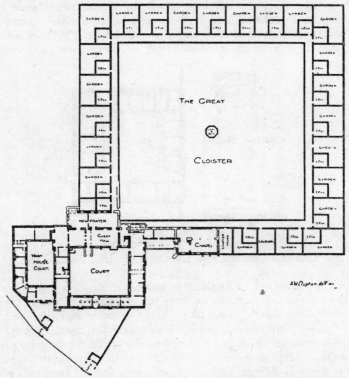

30. LONDON CHARTERHOUSE: Ground Plan. 1371.
Reconstruction by A. W. Clapham. The Great Cloister, including the walk but not the cells, was roughly 300 feet square.

to improve his private practice. This is indicated by the only incident of his life which has survived from this period: a warrant was addressed in 1374 to the keepers of the port of Poole in Dorset ordering them to release from arrest the ship *Margarete* of Wareham, of 48 tons burthen, with two high tombs of marble for the Earl of Arundel and Eleanor his late wife, one great stone for the Bishop of Winchester, and other things of theirs which were on board. The ship, which had been seized for an expedition against France, was to be taken with its contents to London and there unloaded, Master Henry Yevele, "masoun," being the principal surety for this procedure.

This Earl of Arundel and his wife were buried in Lewes Priory; their effigies seem to have been removed at the Dissolution to Chichester Cathedral, where they still remain, though on a modern table-tomb. The general design of this tomb is, however, quite compatible with its representing the scheme of an original by Yevele. No doubt the tombs and the "great stone" for William of Wykeham (whatever this last may have been) were made by the Purbeck marblers to designs by Yevele; from this incident a hint is obtained as to the nature of a part of his work for private clients.

31. LONDON CHARTERHOUSE: Fragment of tomb of Sir Walter Manny
(cusping restored in sketch). 1372.

John of Gaunt returned to England after a disastrous campaign in France in 1373, and began extensive building operations: something was done at Kenilworth Castle, though the main "Lancastrian" work there was not begun for another fifteen years; the great tomb in St. Paul's, for the duke as well as duchess Blanche, was completed, and some repairs were done at the Savoy Palace. The chief craftsman in John of Gaunt's service was the carpenter William Wintringham, who had worked on the great hall roof at Windsor Castle under William Herland, but for masonry works Yevele was consulted, and he and Wintringham were paid £30 for work at the Savoy in 1376. Yevele and Thomas Wreck also had an instalment of £108 for their work on the tomb in St. Paul's, and Yevele's income was still further increased by a grant from the King of the wardship of the manor of Langton in Purbeck, with the issues of the manor from the previous Michaelmas. The grant was to be valid until the coming-of-age of the heiress, Joan, daughter of the late John le Walsh. Langton Matravers is only three miles from Corfe Castle, and here again is a suggestion that Yevele had interests in Purbeck, probably in connection with the stone and marble quarries.

In 1376 Yevele and two other important London masons, Richard atte Churche and Thomas Barnett, were parties to a fine concerning lands in Surrey at Guildford and at Stoke, Send, Crawestoke (Crastock in Woking parish), and Clandon; this may have been an official transaction. The Black Prince died on the 8th of July, after a long illness, and was buried in Canterbury Cathedral. His tomb was erected according to directions left in his will, and it is extremely probable that Yevele was the designer, though no documentary evidence of authorship has yet come to light. Yevele must in any case have been at Canterbury within the next year or so, as his design of the new nave and transepts was ready by the time work began in 1378, under Thomas Hoo, who was resident master mason (66). The consideration of Yevele's work at Canterbury must, however, be left until later.

He was commissioned to impress masons for work at Westminster and the Tower in 1377, the year of the King's jubilee, but there seems to have been little work of importance in progress. The political crisis, brought about by the rivalry between the ecclesiastical faction led by William of Wykeham, and the supporters of John of Gaunt, had lasted for several years, and did nothing to relieve the gloom caused by the reverses suffered in France. The reign, and with it a whole epoch of chequered glory and disaster, closed on the 21st of June, when the old King died at Shene Palace (25). Soon afterwards he was buried in the Sanctuary at Westminster, by the shrine of the royal saint his namesake, and next to his own dead queen.

Chapter III
Fame

THE REIGN OF EDWARD III, IN SPITE OF ITS OVERSHADOWED CLOSE, had been among the greatest in English history, and it was fitting that his monument should be one of the most splendid of those which surrounded the sanctuary of the royal church. The chief artists in the royal service outdid each other in perfecting their respective shares of the work. Yevele was designer of the composition as a whole, and of the body of the tomb. Hugh Herland, who had become chief carpenter two years before, after his father's death, set about the wooden tester of canopy-work and vaulting, the most lovely production of its kind which is known to exist, while the splendid bronze statue of the dead King, with its canopy and angels and the little weepers for the sides of the tomb, were produced by the bronze-founder John Orchard of Knightsbridge, who took a house in Tothill Street, Westminster, to be close to the work. Although the three men used similar motives in their respective parts of the work, the details vary in the stone, wood, and metal sections, and the effect is harmonious without producing monotony. The faces of the King and of the weepers are evident portraits, and all the figures are conceived in a spirited style; considering the occasion, the little statues of the royal children might even be called jaunty (28, 58).

Yevele's design owed something to the adjacent tomb of Queen Philippa, made ten years earlier by Hennequin de Liège, a Fleming working in Paris, but the effect is entirely different, being purely English. The tomb and monument as a whole are the culmination of a type, and even Yevele himself had nothing better to suggest when he came to design a tomb for Richard II and his queen, eighteen years later.

The new reign did not disturb Yevele or his colleagues, and his own office was confirmed to him on the 7th of March following. He was also ordered to take masons to Southampton, where they were to embark with John of Gaunt's expedition to Brittany, which proved a costly failure. The year 1378, though marked by lack of military success, saw the two great ports of Brest and Cherbourg delivered peaceably into English hands, pawned by the Duke of Brittany and the King of Navarre respectively, their owners. Successful French raids on English coast towns gave rise to a state of alarm, leading to the building of new castles and fortifications, and the repair of existing ones. As usual, the Scots joined the French in harassing England, and the next decade was more prolific of castles, mainly on the borders, and in Kent and

Sussex, than any period since the twelfth century, except for the Welsh castle-building under Edward I. On the 1st of October the bailiffs of Canterbury obtained a writ of aid from the Crown, permitting them to impress masons in Kent for the walling of the city, and the operations included the building of the famous West Gate. There is good reason for thinking that Henry Yevele was the designer of this gate, which is not only a formidable defensive work, but also a grand architectural composition (26, 27, 32).

It was at the very same time that the Archbishop, Simon of Sudbury, ordered the clergy of the diocese to collect subscriptions for the rebuilding

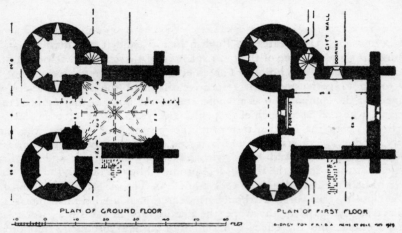

PLAN OF GROUND FLOOR   PLAN OF FIRST FLOOR

32. CANTERBURY WEST GATE: Ground and Upper Plans, measured and drawn by Sidney Toy. 1378.

of the cathedral nave, while he himself paid for the demolition of the Norman building. The work did not at first proceed very fast, but £400 had been spent by the end of 1383, and before the Archbishop's death at the hands of the rebels in 1381, at least some part of the aisle walls had been built (66, 67).

At the beginning of 1379 the City of London raised a loan to effect a reconciliation with the King's Council, and Yevele subscribed 5 marks, or £3 6s. 8d. Later in the year he supplied a new east window for the chancel of St. Mary's Church, Battersea, which belonged to Westminster Abbey, the abbey accounts recording a payment to him of £5 for the work. By this time Yevele was officially master mason to the Abbey, and he had probably held the post since 1373. He could not of course give his full time, and his appointment must have been purely as an architect and consultant. He was paid a yearly fee of £5 for his services, as well as 15s. for a dress and furs. The resident master mason was Robert Kentbury of Westminster.

About this time Yevele seems to have received a commission from much farther afield. John Lord Neville, one of the most important among the northern nobles, wished to provide for Durham Cathedral an altar-screen or reredos worthy of its setting, and decided that the fine work which he required could only be obtained in London. The screen, carved in blocks of Dorset clunch or hard chalk, was made, and transported by sea to New-castle, for land-carriage thence to Durham, in 1380. The style of this work is so like that of the tombs and monuments known to have been designed by Yevele, that it is almost certain that he was responsible. Lord Neville had held many important offices of state, and was in close touch with John of Gaunt, so that Yevele may have been indebted to the latter patron for a recommendation. Very like the work of the Neville Screen at Durham is that of a set of Perpendicular sedilia in Selby Abbey, which too may well have come from Yevele about this time; various works at Selby were certainly in progress soon after 1375 (33, 34, 52).

A work of great importance, the Church and College of Arundel in Sussex, was begun in 1380, and contains many features such as window tracery closely akin to Yevele's style. The College was founded by Richard Fitzalan, Earl of Arundel, son to the earl with whose tomb Yevele had been concerned six years earlier. Comparable to the College at Cobham, that at Arundel was planned to include a completely new church of monastic scale, with central tower. The sternly simple nave is a foil for the exquisite stone pulpit, whose details are almost identical with those of the Cobham sedilia. Arundel and Cobham are unquestionably works of the school of Yevele, even if carried out wholly or in part by others.

Work in the South now began to engage Yevele in a press of business: the city of London decided in view of the danger to shipping in the Thames, to set up a commission to consider the erection of two towers, one on each side of the river. The danger came not only from the French, but from pirates, whose depredations went unchecked until they were captured by a small fleet equipped by the private enterprise of John Philpot, citizen and grocer, in 1378, when he became mayor. Philpot was knighted in 1381 for his courageous behaviour in the face of Wat Tyler, along with William Wal-worth who was then mayor. Walworth was the first of the four commissioners selected in 1380 to decide on the building of defensive towers: the others were John Northampton, another citizen of note; Nicholas Twyford, gold-smith; and Henry Yevele. Yevele, though a prominent citizen and one of the Bridge Wardens, was probably chosen as an expert in military engineering, on the strength of his reputation at Queenborough and Canterbury. Wal-worth himself was to some extent a patron of architecture, for before he died in 1385 he founded a college at the church of St. Michael Crooked Lane, and built a new choir and side-chapels there. This church was close by Yevele's home at the north end of London Bridge, and he may well have been the architect; it will be seen that he had similar work in an adjacent parish in 1381.

During 1380 John Lord Cobham, a member of the great council, obtained licence to crenellate his manor-house at Cooling or Cowling in Kent, some six miles east of Gravesend (38, 62). The desolate peninsula between the Thames and Medway estuaries was dangerously vulnerable, and the Council must have been only too glad to find one of their members undertaking defence works out of his own pocket. Lord Cobham obtained Yevele's services, and plans were ready in the following year when a large contract was let to Thomas Wreck, who had been Yevele's partner in making John of Gaunt's tomb. Wreck had also represented the masons' mistery on the Common Council of London in 1376, and was evidently one of the principal building contractors of the city.

On the 16th of April 1381 Henry Yevele and his colleague William Wynford were present in the chapel of Farnham Castle, when Bishop William of Wykeham received the homage of John de Clere for the lands which the latter held in Crondal, Hants. The two King's masons may have had official business with Wykeham, or possibly both were concerned in the design of his foundation, New College, Oxford. In the same spring of 1381 Yevele had to impress masons for service in Brittany under Thomas Earl of Buckingham, the King's uncle. It was the continuance of these futile expeditions against France which formed the principal drain on the national purse, and led to the heavy Poll Tax which was being collected in the early months of 1381. Incidentally, the French war had also led to a period of comparative stagnation in the arts, for there was no money to spend on purposes unconnected with defence or the prosecution of further and weaker attempts to regain control of the situation across the Channel.

This is not the place to discuss the causes of the great Peasants' Revolt, which sprang from many different forms of discontent, and had perhaps been better prepared than is now generally credited. There certainly were references to a "Great Society" behind the disturbances, and the existence of such a body is not disproved by the fact that the revolt in different places took on a local aspect, and emphasised old grudges which had no connection with the "platform" of the Kentish mob that marched on London. The immediate cause of the disturbances was the collection of the poll-tax, which fell most heavily upon the poor, and the trouble first broke out at Dartford on the 4th of June. Maidstone, Canterbury, and Rochester were immediately the scenes of further risings, and Rochester Castle was taken and sacked on the 6th June. The Kentish men were rapidly gathered into a rabble army under the leadership of "Wat Tyler" and "John Ball," and were encamped on Blackheath by the 12th, entering London on the following day. The rebels directed their attacks against the possessions and supporters of John of Gaunt, the Order of Hospitallers, lawyers, and aliens. Whether by inadvertence or treachery, they were able to enter the Tower on the 14th, and murdered a number of unpopular figures, including Simon of Sudbury, the Archbishop of Canterbury. By this time the situation had got completely out of hand, and the city was in chaos, but the crisis came on Saturday the 15th of June when King Richard, aged fourteen, faced Wat Tyler in Smithfield in front of an immense crowd of rebels, and after a scuffle in which Tyler was arrested and killed by Walworth, mayor of London, saved the situation by telling the mob that he himself was their leader and would see that their grievances were redressed.

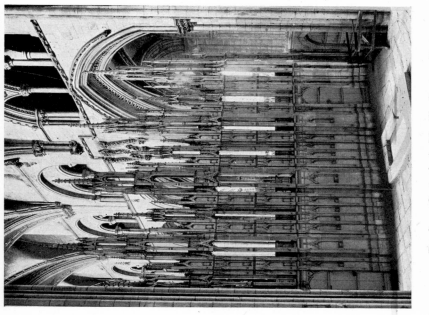

34 Durham Cathedral: Neville Screen from
back. 1379

33 Durham Cathedral: Neville Screen from
West. 1379

S. Petris   3.S. Magnes   2 Gray Church   S Dunston in the East

Billings gate

Lyon key

THE BRIDGE

U S

35 London Bridge and Churches of St. Magnus and St. Dunstan from the South, in 1640
From the engraving by Wenceslaus Hollar, Amsterdam, 1647

UNIVERSITY OF WINNIPEG
PORTAGE & BALMORAL
WINNIPEG 2. MAN.   CANADA

Unfortunately the council overbore the King's wishes, and the rebels were severely dealt with, the general situation being left as it was before the revolt. It is interesting to note that the sympathies of the rebels were from the first in the King's favour, and that meeting the Princess Joan his mother upon the Watling Street, they saluted her with acclamation. Their animus was violent against John of Gaunt, who was conducting negotiations with the Scots upon the Border, fortunately for himself; they also had a grudge against the political civil servants, as was natural, but it is not likely that they interfered with the royal craftsmen, for there were many craftsmen in their own ranks. Hugh Herland had been at Rochester Castle, in charge of extensive repairs, but seems to have come to no harm.

Order was soon restored, and normal life was resumed. At Cowling Castle, a contract for the building of the great gate-house was let to Thomas Crump, a mason of Maidstone, and it was specified that Yevele was to act as quantity surveyor, measuring the work done and certifying the payments due to Crump, as in modern architectural practice. Lord Cobham was taking no chances of arousing hostility among the peasants by the building of the castle, and exhibited on the front of the gatehouse (38). where it may still be read, a notice in English:

> "Knouwyth that beth and schul be
> That I am made in help of the cuntre
> In knowyng of whyche thyng
> Thys is chartre and wytnessyng."

The inscription is in blue enamel on a copper plate, made in the form of a charter with strings and seals.

In December Yevele designed another work for Lord Cobham, but this time it was of quite a different nature, being a new south aisle and porch for the church of St. Dunstan in the East, near Thames Street. The contract was let to Nicholas Typerton, and contained a clause specifying that the work was to be to the design (*la devyse*) of Yevele; this is perhaps the earliest known example of the modern practice in this respect, differentiating clearly the mason-architect from the mason-contractor, who was to develop into the builder of later times. St. Dunstan's perished in the Great Fire, and even Wren's new church has been rebuilt, except for the fine "bow" steeple, one of Wren's Gothic experiments. As it happens, this bears no resemblance to the old steeple, which consisted of a thin needle-spire on a plain battlemented tower. All that can be seen of the south aisle in Hollar's detailed print of "London from Bankside" is the embattled parapet with the heads of the windows below; it seems to have had six bays, inclusive of the porch. How far these arrangements represent Yevele's design is doubtful, for the church underwent a very thorough restoration in 1633, before the date of Hollar's drawing (35).

These works must have occupied a good deal of Yevele's time in 1382, and his visits to Cooling Castle continued at least until 1384, the walls of the castle being completed by a third contractor, William Sharnhale, under a contract of July 1382, for £456. Yevele must also have been busy in connection

7

with the royal marriage in January, and the subsequent coronation of the new queen, Anne of Bohemia. Other work again took Yevele into Kent, for besides the building going on at Canterbury, he was appointed a member of the commission which sat in 1383 to arrange for the building of Rochester Bridge (54). His long experience as Warden of London Bridge, as well as his wide architectural knowledge, here stood him in great stead.

Meanwhile, the demolition of the Norman nave of Westminster Abbey was progressing apace, and the aisle walls and great piers were rising from their new foundations. In spite of the lapse of a century since the building of the five eastern bays of the nave, Yevele adhered to all the main elements of the original design. In so doing he exercised unusual restraint, for mediaeval additions commonly involved a noticeable clash of styles. Unlike the painstaking copyist of latter times, Yevele was too great a creative artist to reproduce the details of the old work, and the result is probably the happiest example in existence of the work of two periods formed into a perfectly harmonious whole. Owing to the long delay which took place before the completion of the nave, it is difficult to tell how far the existing work follows Yevele's designs in detail, but Lethaby was almost certainly right in supposing that the west front and window, as well as the porch, are to be attributed to him, though not actually finished in his lifetime (36, 65). It is a pity that his intentions with regard to the western towers are unknown, for the treatment of the great clasping angle buttresses above the main roof presents a tantalising problem. The sham Gothic towers added by Wren's pupils, though better than none, can only be regarded as a miserable makeshift. It was probably in Yevele's time that a Galilee Porch was added outside the great north door; it had tall three-light windows and narrow buttresses, but it has long been destroyed.

For some time few details of Yevele's life are available, but he was again busy on official work, as in February 1384 he obtained a special protection against forfeiture, for two shops which he held in the parish of St. Martin Outwich, which had once belonged to John Totenham, a city carpenter; the protection was granted on account of the great labours which Yevele "sustained daily" on the King's behalf. He was nevertheless able to take on civic duties, for he was elected one of the two Common Councillors for Bridge Ward in this year, with Thomas Mallyng, another mason. Notwithstanding the King's recognition of his services, he apparently had some difficulty in obtaining payment of his fees, and in 1385 a warrant had to be issued, ordering the payment of his salary of one shilling a day.

In December the bailiffs of Canterbury were granted £100 a year from the issues of Kent, to be expended on the walls of the city under the supervision of John Lord Cobham, two Canterbury burgesses, and Henry Yevele. His connections with Canterbury seem to have been very close during the next ten years, and he must have made the acquaintance of the new archbishop, William Courtenay, if he had not already done so while the latter was Bishop of London between 1375 and 1381. Though a mild reprover of the King's extravagance, the Archbishop was himself an important patron of art and

36 Westminster Abbey: West Front, 1362 and later. The Towers, great window, and niches above porch are not in accordance with Yevele's design

38 Cowling Castle: Outer Gate from without. 1380

37 Saltwood Castle: Great Gatehouse, c. 1383

building. His works included an extensive restoration of the church of Moepham in Kent, the gatehouse of Saltwood Castle near Hythe (37, 39), and the foundation of the new church and college at Maidstone. Both the work at Meopham and the Saltwood gatehouse have the appearance of being Yevele's, and he may well have advised on the buildings at Maidstone, which belong to his school, even if not carried out under Yevele in person.

At Canterbury itself the Prior and Convent of Christchurch Cathedral were in the December of 1386 ordered to carry out repairs to the walls of their close under Yevele's supervision, and during the same year he took part

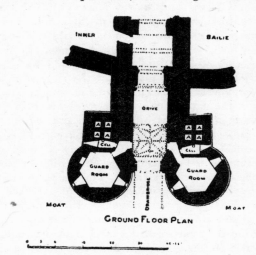

39. SALTWOOD CASTLE: Ground Plan of Great Gatehouse. 1383.
The curtain wall and rear part of gate are earlier.

in an inquiry into the receipts of the ferry service between Rochester and Strood. Evidently Yevele was spending a large proportion of his time in Kent, and so far as official business was concerned this reflected the continued anxiety to improve the defences between the Channel and London. Another outcome of this anxiety was the building of Bodiam Castle just over the Sussex border, some nine miles from Hastings. Licence to crenellate was granted to Sir Edward Dalyngrigge, one of the King's council, in 1385. The position of Dalyngrigge, and the simple, powerful design of the castle, strongly suggest Yevele as the architect, for the building is certainly not the work of an unaided country contractor (63).

From 1384 to 1395 Yevele, as one of the Wardens of London Bridge, was active in the acquisition of properties in Southwark, Lewisham, and Greenwich, and John Clifford, chief mason of the Bridge, was generally associated with him in these transactions. On the 4th of August 1387 Yevele and Clifford, with Sir Robert Knolles, Sir John Cobham (Lord Cobham), and William Rikehille, a justice of the common bench, obtained a recognisance in £360 from nine men of Maidstone and its neighbourhood. Several of these men, Roger and Thomas Crompe, and William Janecoke, are known to have been masons and quarrymen, and this bond must have been to secure performance of a large contract, probably that for the supply of worked stone for the building of Rochester Bridge, where Knolles and Cobham were in charge. The Kentish ragstone and hardstone, quarried in the Maidstone district, was already much used in London for river walls and for the piers of London Bridge.

In 1387–88 Yevele and his second wife Katherine, with William Hochepount chaplain, John Clifford, and Martin Seman clerk (who was later to be one of Yevele's executors), were concerned in the purchase of properties in Southwark, apparently on their own account; perhaps this was the extensive estate near Horsleydown which ultimately descended to William Burgh, heir of Henry's brother Robert, and which was sold by him to Sir John Fastolf in 1447. This estate was just across the river from the Tower of London. Next year Yevele was in charge of the new work at Westminster Abbey, where five of the nave windows were ready for the iron glazing bars. The last of the Norman work was broken down and removed in this year, 1388, and it was possible to visualise the growing nave, free from obstructions. The political scene had once more become stormy: a complicated series of moves and countermoves in 1387 had ended in a rising by Robert de Vere, Earl of Oxford, the King's closest friend, but his forces were completely broken up at Radcot Bridge in Oxfordshire, and the party led by the King's uncle, Thomas of Woodstock, was master of the situation. This party, known as the Appellants from their "appealing" their opponents of treason, forced upon the King the arrest of all his most trusted friends, including his aged tutor, Sir Simon Burley. De Vere had escaped to the Continent, but the rest were tried by a long series of high-handed and illegal processes, and most of them, including Burley, put to death. Queen Anne had made a personal appeal to Thomas of Woodstock, now Duke of Gloucester, for Burley's life but without avail, and the King's lasting resentment at the behaviour of the appellant lords was probably the main cause of his later treatment of his cousin Henry Bolingbroke, who had been one of their number. When, in happier times, a fitting tomb came to be made for Burley in St. Paul's Cathedral, it was a splendid erection, shown by Hollar's view to have been in Yevele's style, and was probably to his designs (61).

The behaviour of the lords appellant had for the time being a serious effect upon the civil service, which they reorganised throughout so far as the clerical officers were concerned. Roger Elmham was made Clerk of the Works, and the controller, William Hannay, who took fees of 1s. 6d. a day, was superseded in favour of one Richard Brundeston, who offered to do the work for 1s. a day. On the pretext of retrenchment of expenditure, all kinds of expedients were resorted to, including some which amounted to rank dishonesty. For example, a sum of £400 was owing to John Lewyn, the great mason, architect, and contractor of Durham, for work he had done at the royal castle of Roxburgh on the Border; instead of payment, Lewyn was granted an allowance of the excess of export duty on wool above £1 per sack, on as much wool as he should export, until the outstanding debt had been cancelled. In other words, Lewyn could only recoup himself by immense exertions in his by-occupation as a wool-merchant, and received not a penny of his money in hard cash. This oppression of the people whom Richard had promised to lead, and the callous indifference shown towards his kingship, met their reward in the summer of 1389, for the King had attained his majority and was able to call the appellants' bluff.

The King was now for the first time in a position to arrange his establishment to suit himself, and in conformity with his artistic tastes. One of the first acts of his personal government was the appointment of Geoffrey Chaucer as Clerk of the Works, on the 12th of July. Chaucer was another sufferer at the hands of the lords appellant, who had deprived him of his pensions. Yevele also had been treated badly, his pay being allowed to fall into arrears, but the new régime contrived to make him less dependent on the Exchequer by granting to him the manors of Tremworth and Vannes, near Wye in Kent, with a cash allowance of 25s. a year to make up the difference in value between the issues of these manors and his old fee of £18 5s. 0d. On the 27th of September Chaucer, as Clerk of the Works, was ordered to pay Yevele all his arrears, and the resumption of official work was marked by the repair of a wharf at the Tower of London. The work was done under contract by Thomas Crump and William Jancook, the Maidstone masons, with John Westcot of London. Yevele was in charge, and though close on seventy, must have been gladdened with the hope of better things to come, now that the King enjoyed his own again.

Chapter IV
The Grand Old Man

RICHARD II'S PERSONAL GOVERNMENT WAS, ARTISTICALLY SPEAK-ing, one of the most brilliant periods in English history; the short space of ten years from 1389 to 1399 was filled with great achievements and included the reconstruction of Westminster Hall, probably the finest piece of domestic work ever built.

The King was determined to refit the royal residences on a new scale of magnificence, and made a beginning with the castle of Winchester, a place with ancient traditions of the English monarchy. On the 3rd of March 1390 the works there were put in charge of a commission of three architects for the term of seven years, the three men being Henry Yevele, William Wynford, and Hugh Herland, the chief carpenter. Wynford, since the completion of the great works at Windsor, had acquired a large private practice, as well as dealing with Crown works in the southern counties, and in 1388 he had begun William of Wykeham's new college buildings at Winchester, where he had made his home. Herland also visited Winchester in connection with Wykeham's carpentry work, so that it was probably unnecessary for Yevele, the eldest of the three, to do more than pay an occasional visit. There is an account still in existence for the following year's work at the castle, and this refers to the "repair and mending of divers defects of the said castle according to the ordering and advice of Henry Yevele and William Wyndford the master masons and Hugh Herland the master carpenter of the said works"; no very large works were done, since only 40 marks (£26 13s. 4d.) were spent in each year. Two months after this appointment Yevele was ordered to supervise repairs to the keep of Canterbury Castle, in conjunction with Hugh Herland, and £200 was granted for the work. The amount of work, pleasant as the change was after the years of gloom, proved to be more than Yevele could combine with his heavy civic responsibilities, and on the 28th of August he obtained an exemption for life from serving on juries or inquests, and from being compelled to hold public offices against his will, in consideration of his being the King's mason and surveyor of the works within the palace of Westminster, the Tower of London, and Castle of Canterbury, as well as on account of his great age.

About 1390 Henry Yevele and William Waddesworth, as Bridge Wardens, sent to Rome to attempt to obtain confirmation of the liberties of the Chapel of St. Thomas on the Bridge. The Chapel had just been rebuilt, in the years

40 Canterbury Cathedral: Cloisters, boss in East walk,
perhaps portrait of Henry Yevele. *c.* 1400

41 Westminster Hall: Interior looking South. 1394.
Designer: Henry Yevele; (of roof) Hugh Herland

since 1384, doubtless to designs by Yevele. The Wardens' emissary, John Pecchee, one of the chaplains of the Bridge Chapel, was met in Rome by a certain John Chircheman, who wrote to Yevele and Waddesworth upbraiding them for not having put the matter into his (Chircheman's) hands, and for having sent Pecchee out without funds. To carry the matter through the Papal Chancery would cost quite £20, and much trouble, but if they were prepared to entrust the business to him, and send the money, he was ready to attempt the matter.[1] Yevele's annoyance upon reading the letter must be left to the imagination.

Another piece of foreign business with which he may have been concerned was the dispatch to Portugal of designs and masons for the Dominican friary of Batalha. This great monastery was founded by John I of Portugal in 1388 to commemorate his great victory over the Spanish at Aljubarrota in 1385, a victory won with the help of English men-at-arms. The alliance had been cemented by the treaty of Windsor in 1386, and by John's marriage to Philippa of Lancaster, daughter of John of Gaunt, in the following year. The remarkable founder's chapel at Batalha, an octagonal lantern enclosed in a square ambulatory, and a church with features reminiscent of the English friars' churches and of Holy Trinity, Hull, and quasi-Perpendicular wall tracery, show that the tradition of English influence is not unfounded, though the principal architect was the Portuguese Affonso Domingues. The aisle windows of the nave of Batalha have tracery so like that of certain of the choir windows at Lichfield, dating from the first half of the century, that one is led to wonder whether "backward" designs were not exported of set purpose to preserve the monopoly of the new English Perpendicular style.

Yevele's first wife Margaret had died at some time between 1384 and 1387, and he had married Katherine, widow of John Hadde of London, known as "Lightfoot." Katherine had a son John and a daughter Elizabeth by her first marriage, and they had been left £40 each by their father in his will, with the proviso that if either of them should die, the whole £80 was to go to the survivor. John Hadde junior had died, and his sister Elizabeth married one William Kyrton, who laid claim to the £80, held in trust by Hadde's executors, John Warner and William Jordan, and Katherine and her second husband Henry Yevele. Unable to obtain the money, William and Elizabeth petitioned against Yevele and his co-trustees before the Mayor and Aldermen at the Guildhall on the 2nd of August 1390, and the parties were summoned to appear on the following day, when the petitioners acknowledged that the debt had meanwhile been satisfied. On the face of it, it might appear that the trustees had been misappropriating the legacies, but in view of Yevele's position this is very unlikely, and the case was probably one of the fictitious suits then common, and simply for the purpose of securing an official enrolment of the receipt.

In December Chaucer paid Yevele arrears amounting to £6 17s. 1d., and early in the following year Yevele gave Chaucer an acknowledgement that he had received payment of all outstanding arrears. Chaucer too had had a

[1] Corporation of London, *Bridge House Deeds*, F. 58 (in French).

busy year, for he had been appointed Clerk of the Works at Windsor as well as in London, had been sitting on a commission for the repair of the banks of the Thames below Greenwich, and had also had to arrange for putting up scaffolds for a great tournament in Smithfield, which took place before the King and Queen in May 1390. He was also writing the later Canterbury Tales, and the Treatise on the Astrolabe for his son Lewis. Chaucer doubtless had to pay frequent visits to Canterbury during the work on the Castle there, and would thus have additional opportunities of obtaining local colour for his masterpiece from fellow-travellers on the road. Yevele was probably a frequent travelling companion of his and may have been the first to hear some of Chaucer's tales, just as Chaucer must have seen Yevele's plans for his great work at Canterbury Cathedral.

Before this Yevele had purchased an estate in Wennington and Aveley in Essex, near Purfleet, and in 1391 he sat on a commission of walls and ditches for the district between Rainham and Aveley. He was able to spend part of his time at this country seat, which was near the Thames, so that he could quickly reach Westminster in comfort by boat, if his presence were required. In the following year he was again a common councillor of London, and in spite of his age took on a heavy additional responsibility as one of the 24 commissioners of the city who went to Nottingham to plead the city's case before the King. King Richard had asked the City for a loan of £1000, which had been refused, and as a result the mayor and a number of officials were arrested, and the civic liberties suspended from May to September. Sir Edward Dalyngrigge was made warden of London, and it was only at the end of the summer that the King received the city back into his favour, as a result of the pleadings of the 24 burgesses and the intercession of Queen Anne. When the news reached London that the King had relented and was returning, a great reception was prepared, and the King and Queen passed through the streets to Westminster amid acclamations, while official deputations presented them with wine from golden cups, golden crowns of fine workmanship, and two paintings of great value. Never before had an English sovereign been received with such honours, and the elaborate arrangements and decorations were no doubt contrived to suit the royal taste by the King's own chief architect, Henry Yevele, in his other capacity as the principal architect among the citizens.

In the following February it was again ordered that Yevele should oversee the repairs to the "dongeon" or keep of Canterbury Castle, but he was certainly in London for a considerable part of the year, as a kitchen account of William of Wykeham shows that Yevele was the Bishop's guest at Winchester House in Southwark on nine occasions between the 29th of April and the 3rd of July[1] (42–45). These visits may indicate simply a friendship of long

[1] For permission to include this very interesting information I am indebted to Mr. Herbert Chitty, F.S.A., the discoverer, and to the Warden and Fellows of Winchester College, who have allowed entries including the names of Yevele and Wynford to be reproduced from the roll for this book. It is to be hoped that circumstances will permit Mr. Chitty's projected edition of this unique document to be published without undue delay, as it throws much light on the daily domestic and social relationships of many of the important figures of the time.

Kitchen Account, 5th May (1393). Yevele a guest at Winchester House, Southwark, where he met Thomas Poynings, Lord St. John of Basing, and Nicholas Stoket, rector of his own parish church of St. Magnus. For translation of entry see p. 53.

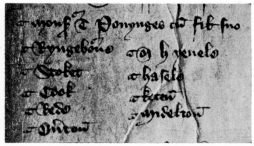

Enlargement from above

My Lord T. Ponynges with his son

Ryngebourne	Mr. H. Yevele
Stoket	Hasele
Cook	Keten
Rede	Midelton
Overton	

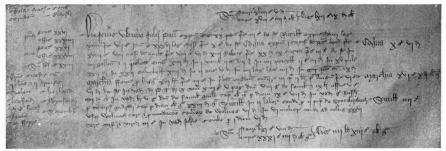

Kitchen Account, Thursday, 31st July (1393), Herland, Wynford and Simon Membury among guests, presumably at Wolvesey Palace, Winchester

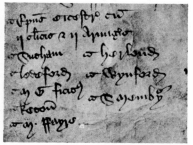

Enlargement from above

The Bishop of Chichester with 2 clerks and 2 esquires

Sutham	Herlond
Ledeford	Wynford
Mr. G., Physician	S. Membury
Keton	
M. Fayre	

42–45 Winchester College: Household Account Roll of Bishop William of Wykeham, April–September 1393; entry showing Yevele as Wykeham's guest on 5th May; and entry showing Hugh Herland, William Wynford and Simon Membury as guests on 31st July, during a visit paid to Wykeham by Richard Mitford, Bishop of Chichester. See pp. ix, x.

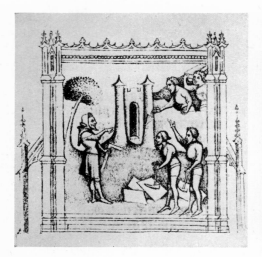

46 A Master Mason, holding square, directing the building of a castle. Two hewers, with axes and stones, are in the foreground, while a labourer carries a block of dressed ashlar to the setter, above, who holds a trowel

47 A fourteenth-century drawing office. The tracing-board rests on its own trestles; the standing figure pointing to a scroll is probably the Master Mason; and the draughtsman his assistant

48 Winchester College: Chapel, East Window. Portraits of the Carpenter (Hugh Herland); Mason, William Wynford; and Clerk of Works, Simon Membury. 1393

standing, but Yevele's professional advice would have been most valuable to Wykeham at a time when the Bishop was contemplating the resumption of work on the new nave of Winchester Cathedral. There is a close relationship between the work at Winchester, which was designed by William Wynford, and the style of Yevele, but this would be a probable consequence of the close association of the two architects in the same department. Among Wykeham's guests present on the occasion of Yevele's visits were Chief Justice Charlton and Justice Thirning, Thomas Poynings Lord St. John of Basing, John Lord Lovell, and the Priors of Southwark and Winchester. Lord Lovell in this same year of 1393 obtained licence to build a castle at Wardour in Wiltshire; the remarkable hexagonal plan is suggestive of Queenborough, but the detail was more probably designed by Wynford than by Yevele.

Another document preserved by chance, the day-book of Gybon or Gilbert Maghfield, a London merchant, shows that in 1393 Yevele purchased millstones from Maghfield, who was at the time one of the sheriffs of the city. Presumably these millstones were required for one of Yevele's country properties, or more probably for the water-mills on his property near Horsleydown in the parish of St. Olave, Southwark. He was still a Warden of the Bridge in 1394 and 1395, and in April 1394 was a party to a property transaction in Gracechurch Street, the northward continuation of Fish Street Hill.

By this time his last great work had been begun: the reconstruction of Westminster Hall. The old hall had been built by William Rufus about 1097–99, and was an enormous building, 238 feet long and 69 feet wide (41, 57). It was, however, encumbered with two ranges of great posts which were needed for the support of the roof, the hall being divided into three aisles. The walls were pierced by Norman windows, with a continuous arcading and a passage in the thickness of the wall. Remarkable as the old hall was in its time, it must have seemed heavy and awkward to Richard II, who required that the great hall of his chief palace should be the most beautiful and the most up-to-date that could be made. He had been considering its rebuilding for some time, and in the summer of 1393 the clerk of the works (John Gedney, who had succeeded Chaucer in 1391) was ordered to have timber brought from the King's wood at Petley in Sussex to the palace.

The design for the reconstruction was prepared in 1393 and 1394, by Yevele and Hugh Herland, for the new masonry and carpentry works respectively. It was decided that the shell of the old hall should be retained, but that it should be re-worked and re-cased in such a way as to appear entirely new. The old wall-passage and windows were to disappear, and a new range of traceried windows was to be made on each side. Beneath the windows the design provided for a string-course enriched with carvings of the White Hart, the King's badge, and above them for a new cornice to take the wall-plate at the lower end of the roof-timbers. The north or entrance end of the hall was provided with a porch flanked by square towers (23), and behind the dais at the south end was a great window and on each side of it three statues of kings in canopied niches (41).

8

Yevele's genius for simplicity combined with beautiful composition and
massing made of the hall a perfect foil for the rich detail of Herland's lovely
roof above. It is of course Herland's roof which is the special and indeed
unique feature of the hall, spanning with a single arch a space which had previously been divided into three with heavy posts, but this *tour-de-force* of

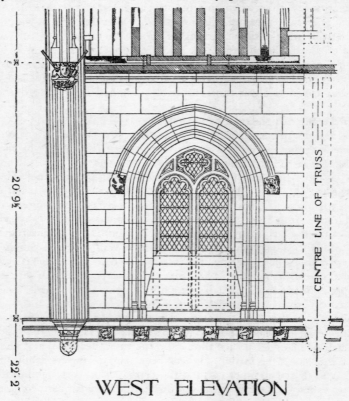

WEST ELEVATION

SCALE FOR
BAY

49. WESTMINSTER HALL: side window, corgel-course and cornice. 1394.

design tends to cause Yevele's share to be overlooked. Yevele was of course
a genius of the very highest rank, and he never showed this more truly than
in accepting the thirteenth-century outlines at Westminster Abbey, and in
subordinating the stone walls of the hall to his colleague's wonderful roof,
which he recognised as the crown of the whole work.

The rebuilding began in earnest at the beginning of 1394, when John
Godmeston was appointed clerk of the works of the hall, and Hugh Herland

was made controller to him for the repairs. Soon afterwards orders were sent out for the purchase of lead, and freestone was obtained from Marr in Yorkshire, near Doncaster. Everything was in train for actual building to begin, when the whole course of events was changed by tragedy. Queen Anne died suddenly at Shene Palace on the 7th of June, aged only twenty-seven. King Richard was so deeply attached to her that he became for a short time practically insane, ordering the demolition of Shene Palace in a fit of frenzy. He soon afterwards left for Ireland on an expedition which he had long projected, and did not return until the May of 1395. Before his return the King sent orders for the work at Westminster to be proceeded with, and a contract for the new cornice, corbels, and ashlar-work was let to two Gloucestershire masons, Richard Washbourn and John Swallow, on the 18th of March. They were to execute the cornice "according to the purport of a pattern and mould made by the advice of Master Henry Yeveley and delivered to the said masons by Watkin Walton his warden," and Master Henry and "Watkyn" were to view the twenty-six corbels and pass them as satisfactory. The whole of this work was to be finished by the 2nd of February 1396.

Meanwhile Yevele had been at work on an important tomb in Westminster Abbey for Cardinal Langham, who had been buried there in 1388—Langham had died in 1376, but his body was not brought to Westminster for twelve years. In this work he had as junior partner the mason Stephen Lote, a man of Kent whom he may have met in Canterbury, and who first appeared in London, in the Queen's employ, in 1390. Yevele and Lote received an instalment of £20 for Langham's tomb in the spring of 1395, and on the 1st of April they undertook a more important contract, for the tomb of the King and Queen. This was to be finished by Michaelmas 1397, and they were to be paid £250, with an extra £20 if the King were pleased with the result.

Langham's tomb is of a single stage, and is decorated with the same motive of elaborated and cusped quatrefoils which appears on the lower stages of the tombs of Edward III and Richard II (59). The latter tomb closely follows the design of that of Edward III, but is broader, to contain the coffins of the King and Queen, and to leave space for their figures, which originally had their hands clasped together in token of their undying love (53). The images were made by two London coppersmiths, Nicholas Broker and Godfrey Prest.

The masonry work of the hall had been proceeding rapidly, and was apparently ready for the roof-timbers in 1395; when the new Queen Isabella was crowned on the 7th of January 1397, the roof was already structurally complete, but had to be given a temporary covering for the festivities. The north front with its towers and porch was being pushed forward, but the building was only finished in 1400, the year of Yevele's death.

The year 1395 was the last in which he served as Warden of London Bridge, and he apparently did not undertake any more new works, though about this time he may have made sketches or given advice upon the new church and college which Archbishop Courtenay was founding at Maidstone. The great works at Westminster Abbey and Hall, and at Canterbury Cathedral, must have required all the energy he possessed, and Watkin or Walter Walton his warden evidently acted as his chief assistant to lessen the burden. Walton had been a prominent London mason since the early 1380's, and after 1394 he seems to have stood in a special relation to Yevele as the great master's deputy, being commissioned to impress masons for the repair of Portchester Castle in 1396, and receiving an appointment in the following year as "chief surveyor of the stone-cutters and masons for the King's works in England."

It is a remarkable fact that both Yevele and Hugh Herland were old men at the time that they designed Westminster Hall, one of the most vital monuments ever built. Both had had long careers, having reached a high degree of success early in middle life, both had poured themselves out in a torrent of creative art for a whole generation long, and yet were together able to rise to supreme heights when they had almost reached their allotted span. They belonged to that class of grand old men which is typical of ripe but yet virile societies: men such as Aeschylus, Sophocles, and Euripides, Giotto, Leonardo da Vinci and Titian, Bach, Handel, Haydn and Goethe. Such men are not only endowed with genius of far higher quality than that of the common run of mankind, but they actually have it in greater quantity too, and often add great physical strength to their other gifts.

Henry Yevele was a man of this stamp, and was producing a masterpiece when he was well past seventy, but it was not to be expected that he could do more. Like Haydn, and perhaps it is not altogether fanciful to compare him to the father of the symphony, Yevele was to have a few years of sunny evening after his great exertions, and then, again like Haydn, was to die in the midst of a political convulsion, though fortunately not to the sound of artillery. The period of quiescence began in 1396, when he was a member of the *Salve Regina* fraternity at St. Magnus; Stow gives an account of the origin of this guild: "The better sort of the Parish to the honour of God and his glorious Mother caused to be made a chantry to sing an anthem of our Lady called *Salve regina* every evening, and ordained five burning wax lights at the time of the said anthem in reverence for the five principal joys of our Lady and for exciting the people to devotion." Yevele had prepared his own tomb in the Chapel of St. Mary in St. Magnus, and it existed there until the Great Fire; another tomb which he may have designed towards the close of his life is that of Rahere in the priory church of St. Bartholomew the Great. It is a beautiful and mature work, closely resembling Langham's tomb in Westminster Abbey, but it is still surrounded by its beautiful screen and canopy-work, which Langham's has lost (60).

The year 1397 saw the success of the King's patient planning for a lasting peace with France, when the young Queen Isabella was crowned; later came the plot of the Duke of Gloucester, and the earls of Arundel and Warwick, followed by Arundel's trial and execution, Warwick's exile, and Gloucester's mysterious death in prison at Calais. This plot, and the political capital which seems to have been made out of the execution of the popular earl of Arundel, was among the principal causes leading to the revolution two years later, though by 1398 it seemed that what was left of the old party of

Appellants had been finally extinguished, and there was every reason to hope for a long period of peace and prosperity. In February 1397 the seven-years appointment of the commission for repairs at Winchester Castle had been renewed for a second term of the same length, Yevele, Wynford and Herland being re-appointed as overseers of the work. No further mention of Yevele occurs for eighteen months, and he was probably spending a greater proportion of his time in the country, for he next appears at Wennington in Essex on the 29th of July 1398, as witness to a deed relating to property in the district. Another witness was Stephen Lote, who also had obtained land there. At Christmas, both Yevele and Lote received robes as esquires of the Prior of Christchurch, Canterbury, and it seems probable that Lote was carrying on Yevele's Canterbury practice in the same way that Walton was deputising in connection with official works, while John Clifford had taken over his work for London Bridge, and William Colchester was apparently his understudy at Westminster Abbey. These four men were the principal members of Yevele's "school" and after his death played a considerable part in spreading his style over the country, both directly and by their contacts.

During the last two years of Richard II's reign, Yevele's great works were rapidly approaching completion; Westminster Hall was in fact structurally finished, and was receiving its final embellishments and carvings; the Abbey nave was approaching its full height in some bays, and at Canterbury the nave vaulting was being built (66). It is to be hoped that Yevele was able to visit his buildings often enough to see their growth towards completion and how nearly they achieved perfection of form. He was, of course, very well off, deriving an income from many properties of his own, as well as from the manors in Kent which were his for life, and from his professional engagements. In these last years from 1397 to 1399, he must have been able to live the life of a country gentleman or city magnate, as he pleased, enjoying a well-earned leisure, occupied with his crowded memories and the solace of his religion. The spirit expressed in his church works is that of a deeply religious man, free both from the scepticism which was growing in his own time, and from the morbidity which was soon to overtake the religious art of Western Europe in the critical fifteenth century.

This peaceful autumn in a prosperous country under an art-loving King must have recalled the bright days of his boyhood and youth, before the scene had been darkened by the French war, the pestilence, and the economic troubles which had produced the Peasants' Revolt. There seemed hardly a cloud on the horizon, and every reason to predict for the King a long and glorious reign, and for English art a further period of development under the new generation, who could begin where Chaucer, Yevele, and their contemporaries were leaving off.

It was not to be; the greatest tragedy in English history was preparing, a tragedy which was not only to deluge the country in blood for a century to come, but was to transfer the real power from the hands of the King, whose interests in the long run always lay with the people's, to those of the magnates, who were very often actuated by purely selfish motives. Early in 1398 came the fatal quarrel between Gaunt's son Henry, and Thomas Mowbray, earl of Nottingham and newly created duke of Norfolk. Strong suspicion of treason rested on both, and after trial by combat had actually begun near Coventry on the 16th of September, the King stopped the battle and banished both the combatants, Henry for ten years, and Norfolk for life. King Richard had realised the impossibility of giving to the country the inestimable benefits of stable government and security, so long as the scales of justice were weighed down with the power of great nobles, and the administration was liable to periodical upsets through political log-rolling.

True to mediaeval doctrine and mediaeval thought, the King did not imagine that any person could or would contest his supreme rights as Monarch, or would dare to advance any conflicting claims as of right. When John of Gaunt died in February 1399 the King decided to confiscate his vast estates, and in view of the fact that the heir had been exiled for treason no other course was reasonably possible. An opportunity had arrived to bring the whole kingdom under the King's control; the existence of the Lancastrian estates and their Palatine jurisdiction were grave menaces to the safety of the realm. Unfortunately, at this critical time a second expedition to Ireland was made necessary by the failure of the Irish chiefs to honour their obligations, and by the murder of the lieutenant, the earl of March. Trusting to his divinely appointed right, the King left England at the end of May, but was almost immediately followed by news of the invasion of England by Henry of Lancaster. What ensued is common knowledge; the King's betrayal, first in Ireland by the false advice of his cousin Edward, whom he had created duke of Albemarle, and later by Archbishop Arundel at Conway, led to his deposition in favour of Henry, who had no valid claim to the Crown whatsoever. Henry, who had already committed treason and sacrilege by taking up arms against his anointed sovereign, did not scruple to have him murdered, apparently by starvation, some time early in February 1400.

The shocking events of the autumn of 1399 seem to have brought Yevele back to London, but instead of living at his house beside St. Magnus, he crossed the bridge into Southwark, where in February 1400 he obtained licence for himself and Katherine his wife to hear service in his private chapel. He was evidently quite infirm and unable to move about much, and on the 25th of May he made his will. He appointed John Clifford and Stephen Lote, his wife Katherine, Richard Parker his cousin, and Martin Seman clerk, to be his executors, and John Warner alderman as overseer. He left his extensive properties to his wife on condition that she should maintain two chaplains to celebrate mass at the altar of St. Mary in St. Magnus' Church for the souls of Margaret his first wife, his parents Roger and Marion, King Edward III, Sir John Beauchamp and others. His omission of King Richard II probably implies that like so many others, he was unable to believe in the King's death. The Sir John Beauchamp referred to was probably the standard-bearer of Crécy, a foundation knight of the Garter, whose tomb in St. Paul's was long known as "Duke Humphrey's"; this tomb may have been designed by Yevele (50).

His property included several tenements, two quays and a brewery called "La Glene" in the parish of St. Magnus, other houses in Basing Lane and Cordwainer Street in the parish of St. Martin Outwich, watermills and houses in Southwark in the parish of St. Olave, his estate in Wennington and Aveley, Essex, and lands at Deptford and Greenwich which he held jointly with John Clifford. The revision of the property went to the Church of St. Magnus upon certain trusts, and failing that to the maintenance of London Bridge and of two chantry priests in the Bridge Chapel. Among properties which were later held by the Bridge, was his tenement "situate between the King's road on the east and the Oyster Gate on the west," which at one time belonged to the *Salve Regina* fraternity. This house was at the north end of the bridge, opposite the church of St. Magnus. Part of the residue of Yevele's estate was to be devoted to the rebuilding of the ancient aisle in the church of the Hospital of St. Thomas the Martyr of Southwark, "where the poor inmates lie."

On the 7th of June Yevele gave letters of Attorney to John Clifford to deliver seisin of some property at Greenwich of which they were then disposing; less than three months later he died, on the 21st August, his will being proved on the 12th of September; Chaucer followed him a few weeks later. Henry Yevele was laid in the tomb he had prepared at St. Magnus; Lote and Clifford had his name and the date inscribed, with the very modest boast that he had been Freemason to three Kings, Edward III, Richard II, and Henry IV, and there, awaiting the Resurrection, they left him. Winter was coming on, and the glory of mediaeval England and the fourteenth century departed together.

WYKEHAM'S HOUSEHOLD ROLL, 1393; TRANSLATION OF ENTRY OF 5 MAY (42).

MONDAY 5 MAY: Pantry—consumed 200 loaves price 3s. 9d. from stock. Buttery—consumed 13 gallons of wine price 6s. 6d. Also consumed 102 gallons of ale price 8s. 6d. from stock. For 2 gallons of wine bought 1s. 4d. *Kitchen*—consumed 1 quarter of beef price 4s., 1 (carcase) of bacon price 2s., 1½ carcases of mutton price 3s., 5 capons price 1s. 8d., from stock. For 3 fowls bought 7½d. For 5 piglets 2s. 8d. For 1½ (carcases) of veal bought 4s. 1d. For 4 lambs 3s. 4d. For doves 1s. 4d. For 19 chickens 2s. 4d. 250 eggs bought 1s. 6d. For porterage 1d. For the expenses of R. Farnham, R. Esshe and 4 other grooms and pages of the kitchen (coming) from Farnham to Ash and thence to London 1s. 2d. *Stables*—Hay for 50 horses 21 mules (?). price 4s. For their feed 3 quarters 3 bushels 1 peck of oats price 6s. from stock. For the wages of T. Ropp, T. Somer, 14 grooms, 5 pages of the lord, 9 grooms of the household and 1 man of T. Wayte 4s. 8d.

dinner ..gentles 23
    ..officers 31

supper ..gentles 18
    ..officers 36

Total messes 108

Lord T. Ponynges
with his son
Ryngebourne
Stoket   Mr. H. Yevele
Cook   Hasele
Rede   Keton
Overton Midelton

Buttery 1s. 4d.

Kitchen
17s. 1½d.

Stables 4s. 8d.

Total $\begin{cases} \text{stock} & \text{£1 19s. 5d.} \\ \text{purchases} & \text{£1 3s. 1½d.} \end{cases}$ Diet £3 2s. 6½d.

Chapter V
Yevele and His Work

IN TURNING FROM THE NARRATIVE OF YEVELE'S LIFE TO A CONsideration of his work, I am conscious of leaving the firm ground of fact and the solid scaffolding of rational conjecture, to tread the quagmire of personal opinion. Taste in architecture, even more than in the other arts, undergoes great and comparatively frequent revolutions, and to the follower of Ruskin (who thought the Perpendicular style "detestable") or of Wren (who cherished the good "Roman manner"), the works of Yevele may make little appeal. In passing, it is only fair to recall that the particular point which Ruskin was discussing when he declared Perpendicular to be detestable, was the suppression of wall-surfaces. Now of all the English architects, Yevele perhaps loved plain walling the most, so much so that Lethaby, who loved his memory, felt that his style was big and bare. I think that this conveys a false impression, but it does contain the germ of Yevele's essential qualities: he was big, in the sense that his conceptions were on a grand scale, and he was bare because he made the whole a thing greater than the sum of its parts, and scorned the meretricious effect of ornament for its own sake, an error into which his successors undoubtedly fell.

The remarkable thing about Yevele, and it is the very kernel of his greatness, is that he did for our architecture what Chaucer did for our language, giving to it a special character which was altogether national, even though it was part of a common European heritage, like the other arts and sciences. Before the Black Death, the difference between French and English architecture had been one of degree rather than of kind, and the truly English fundamentals were to be found in plan and massing and proportion rather than in that mysterious attribute which is termed style. Just so the Anglo-Norman dialect of the English Court differed from the French of France, being overlaid upon a people who thought in Teutonic constructions. So far as language goes, the same difference can be heard between the English of England, and the English language now spoken by most of the people of Ireland—the bones of Celtic thought still protrude in places from the Saxon skin, but Anglo-Irish is nevertheless a form of the English language.

Just as the inherent strength of English at last found expression in Chaucer, and produced a new literature which was not French, yet was thoroughly rooted in European culture, so did the ancient traditions of English building come to fruition in the work of Yevele, who provided a new architectural

54

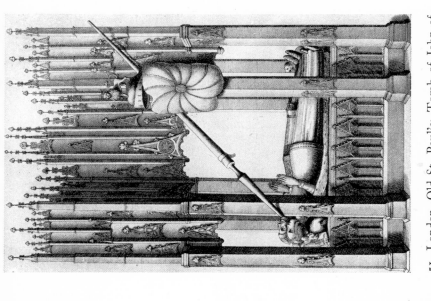

51 London, Old St. Paul's: Tomb of John of
Gaunt and Duchess Blanche of Lancaster,
1374, from an engraving after Hollar

50 London, Old St. Paul's: Tomb of Sir John Beauchamp,
K.G., *c.* 1360, from an engraving after Hollar. The design
of the tomb for the Earl of Arundel, 1373 (modern copy
now in Chichester Cathedral) is almost identical

53 Westminster Abbey: Tomb of Richard II from South-west. 1395

52 Selby Abbey: Sedilia, c. 1375. The spires are restorations

idiom in which those traditional ideas could be expressed. The new idiom of Yevele did not have the same luck as the language of Chaucer, being cut off after a bare 150 years. The comparison can best be visualised by supposing the English language to have been suppressed by Philip II, with the result of making England a Spanish-speaking country for over two hundred years, and Shakespeare and all his successors as far as Byron never to have written. If that had really happened, English literature would have a "prehistoric" beginning, a Golden Age of Chaucer and Gower, followed by the prolific but pedestrian output of Lydgate, Occleve and their kindred, and would have ended tantalisingly with the magnificent promise of Caxton, Malory and Skelton.

It may be objected that such a development is unthinkable, but the downfall of English architecture would be quite as unthinkable if it had not actually happened. All that can be done now is to study the truncated fragment which time has spared, to appreciate its beauty, and to learn the lessons it can teach the present and the future. If English literature had been cut short in the way outlined above, Chaucer would overshadow all the rest, and the study of Chaucer would be the main subject for those who planned any reconstruction of English literature. In the same way I suggest that the study of Yevele should in actual fact be the first care of those who desire to build up a new and sincere English architecture, rooted in the past, yet fitted for the changed conditions of the present. The archaic phrasing of Chaucer and the archaic detail of Yevele are not essential, and can be modified, but the living spirit of their works is a clear fountain of the running waters of truth.

It is a commonplace that the Gothic Revivalists went astray, and it appears to be generally agreed that they were wrong in attempting a revival at all, but it seems to me that their basic theory was perfectly correct, however wrong they may have been in practice. When things are found to be going wrong in any department of life, it is a sound rule to cast back into the past for some point of comparison, and for all that may be discovered of the relics of tradition. The Revivalists cast back, but their aim and judgment were poor; first, they chose as their model a period, the Early English, when native genius had not fully adapted the lessons learnt from France; they then applied the details of their chosen period to modern uses without modification, and made things worse by accepting as normal for civic and domestic work, details and enrichments which in the thirteenth century were only used in expensive church work. Such methods could lead to nothing but failure and what was worse, to a general contempt for Gothic architecture.

Another but smaller group came nearer to the truth almost by accident; instead of plunging back to the time when English art was only just becoming distinct from French, they tried to begin where Gothic left off, and produced some very passable specimens of "neo-Perpendicular," such as the London Guildhall Library, and one masterpiece, the new Houses of Parliament. By the accidental proximity of Henry VII's Chapel, the most florid Tudor style was adopted, with remarkably happy results, but it is a pity that the equally if not more appropriate style of Westminster Hall itself was not chosen instead. It is indeed curious that it was not, for it would have been more reasonable to copy what was left of the old palace, than to match a part of the Abbey across the way; moreover, where Barry and Pugin were not tied down by the official conditions, as in the internal courtyards, they showed that they had managed to capture a trace of the strength and dignity which belonged to Yevele and his school.

Before the art of Yevele and his colleagues can be properly understood, it will be necessary for drawings and photographs of all their works to be brought together to form a corpus of architecture for the period. The fullest detail and adequate description of materials and colour-decoration will have to be given, as well as the mere forms of the work. I can only hope that architecture will be able to produce as definite and scholarly editions of the works of Yevele, Wynford, the Herlands, and others, as the late Professor Skeat did of Chaucer and Langland. In the meantime it is possible to learn something from repeated visits to the monuments themselves, and by examination of the large quantities of scattered illustrations which do exist. I have not been able to visit every one of Yevele's extant works for lack of time and opportunity, and I cannot therefore claim that the following notes are authoritative; defini-tive they certainly are not. But they will have served their purpose if they inspire others with the desire to know more of Yevele, and the determination to improve upon this necessarily tentative criticism.

It is first of all necessary to set some standard of authenticity, comparable to the tests of the textual editor. Yevele's genuine works may be divided into two main groups: those where his authorship rests on positive docu-mentary evidence, and those whose attribution depends on style alone, or upon a combination of style with other circumstances which render Yevele's authorship probable. Both classes can further be subdivided into the extant and the destroyed. Before going further I will mention that there are certain serious critics who consider that mediaeval craftsmen have been wrongly credited with the design of the works they built, and that the real architects of the Middle Ages are still to be sought among the ranks of the clerical civil servants (such as William of Wykeham) and men of comparable standing in private life. This is not the place for a general discussion of the position, but so far as the mediaeval office of works is concerned, there is one piece of evidence which appears to me conclusively against the clerical theory, at any rate after the late thirteenth century; whereas the master craftsmen held office for long terms and generally for life, the clerics came and went, dodging from post to post with the greatest indifference, and seldom held such offices as that of clerk of the King's works for more than five or six years. This suggests, not that clerical promotion was the reward of the successful architect, but that architectural posts were sometimes steps in the ladder of clerical pro-motion.

Fortunately, Yevele is one of the few master craftsmen of whose architectural status there is clear evidence: the contracts for a new aisle and porch at St. Dunstan's in the East, and for the new masonry work in Westminster Hall both state that the work was to be made according to Yevele's design, or to a

54 Rochester Bridge from downstream. 1383

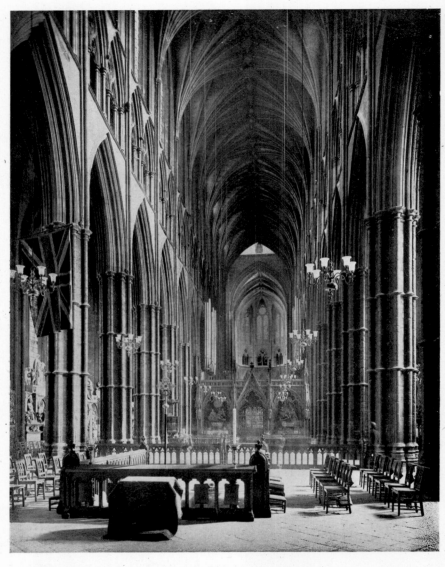

55 Westminster Abbey: Nave looking East. 1362 and later. The Nave
is harmonised with the 13th-century work farther East

pattern made by his advice. Of the two works thus authenticated, only one survives, but that one is among his greatest, and shows his style in its final maturity. Since Yevele did undoubtedly design these two works, which were erected on an almost exact counterpart of the modern contract system, and at least one of them was a work of the very highest importance, there can be little danger in assuming that he also designed all those works which he is known to have built, or which were made by his advice. Further, there will be a strong case in favour of his authorship of all works in connection with

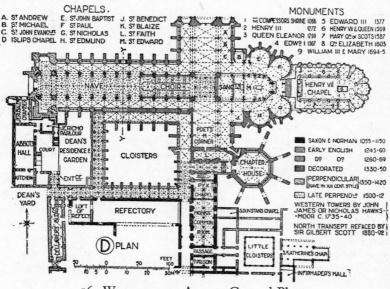

56. WESTMINSTER ABBEY: Ground Plan.

which his name is mentioned, always providing that this does not conflict with the style of the buildings or monuments themselves. Lastly come works where his name is not mentioned at all, but which resemble his known work in greater or less degree.

Henry Yevele was both a prolific and a versatile master, and it is necessary to arrange his works according to some natural classification apart from that of their dates. It is as though Chaucer had written plays, or Shakespeare prose, in addition to their actual output, for Yevele practised all the branches of the mistress art, domestic, military, ecclesiastical, and monumental, which might be likened to prose, drama, and epic and lyric poetry. Dealing with his work in this order, the first building known is his contract at Kennington Manor in 1358; this is lost, and has left no trace. Four years later came the planning of the Abbot's House (later Deanery) at Westminster. The part of this which remains consists of the chamber, hall and kitchen, all in one straight range running from North to South. The Abbot's (Jerusalem) Chamber

overlaps the south-western tower of the church, and is thus narrower than
the hall, though their western walls are in one line. It communicates with
the hall by a lobby at its south-east corner, now of later work. The hall
itself is a finely proportioned room lit by tall two-light windows with traceried
heads, which are of particular interest as the earliest of Yevele's tracery now
known, except for that of the west cloister which it much resembles. The
principal divisions form one "straight-sided" reticulation in the head; this
opening is subdivided saltire-wise, so as to produce a cross of unequal-lobed
quatrefoils above the heads of the two lights, which have cinque-foiled
cusping of the blunted variety. Externally, the walls are a plain face of
masonry, broken only by these windows and their label-moulds (20). The
walls to the street are now surmounted by an embattled cresting, which
may represent the original work, for a similar cresting appears in a pen-and-ink
sketch by Hollar.

The Abbot's House represents what is essential in a mediaeval dwelling,
and its quiet restraint and beautifully proportioned parts are completely
satisfying. Another simple work of Yevele's early period was the famous
palace clock-tower of 1365, long ago destroyed, but known from views by
Hollar and others. It was a strictly functional building, a plain tower apparently
of smooth ashlar masonry, rising two storeys above the surrounding buildings;
the lower of these stages was occupied by the clock, and the upper by the
bells. The three-light windows in the top stage seem to have had tracery
with straight-sided reticulations, the form which Yevele used again and again,
in many variants (24). A clock-tower of closely similar design still stands
in the town of St. Albans; this was perhaps built by Thomas Wolvey of St.
Albans, one of the principal contractors who worked under Yevele at Westminster Hall.

From 1365 onwards Yevele was connected with London Bridge, but the
works there called for steady maintenance rather than design, except for the
rebuilding of the Bridge Chapel,[1] but he was still engaged on the Abbot's
House at Westminster up to 1376, together with other domestic buildings
at the Abbey, such as the Cellarer's range alongside Dean's Yard (19). In
1372 Yevele designed and built a small bridge between Chelmsford and
Moulsham for the Abbot of Westminster, but this is lost. Four years later
he carried out extensive works at the Savoy for John of Gaunt, but these
were destroyed in 1381 when the peasant mob sacked the palace.

Two other works of quasi-domestic character with which Yevele was
probably concerned were the Colleges at Cobham, Kent, begun in 1370,
and at Arundel, Sussex, started ten years later. The Cobham plan is perhaps
the first example of its type, and may well have been inspired by Yevele's
contemporary work on the London Charterhouse. If so, Yevele is to be
regarded as the originator of the typical college plan adopted at Oxford and
Cambridge in the following century, and in part also derived from his
colleague Wynford's work on the State Apartments of Windsor Castle, and
at Winchester and New College, Oxford. The Cobham hall windows employ

[1] For this Chapel, see Gordon Home: *Old London Bridge*, 1931.

a simple pattern of early Perpendicular tracery which is repeated in the chapter house at Canterbury in a more mature form.

In 1383 Yevele designed the new stone bridge over the Medway at Rochester which superseded a much earlier timber structure. Excepting only London Bridge itself, this was the most important bridge in the country, and formed a vital link on the direct road to Canterbury and Dover. After surviving for nearly five centuries, Yevele's fine work was replaced by modern vandals with an iron atrocity of the worst description. Much as we may regret the disappearance of old London Bridge, its successor is at least a fine specimen

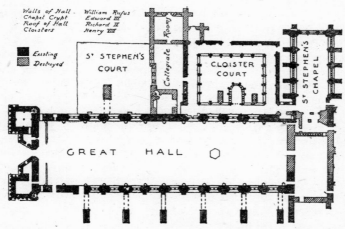

57. WESTMINSTER PALACE: Plan of Hall and St. Stephen's College. The Hall is 238 feet long and 69 feet wide internally, and the span of St. Stephen's Chapel is 34 feet.

of its own period, but at Rochester we have not even that small consolation. Yevele's bridge was a substantial stone structure, fourteen feet wide, and was completed in 1392 (54).

A piece of work which must be included as domestic, for want of a better term, was the new wharf built at the Tower of London in 1389; Yevele had expert knowledge of this type of work, since he owned two quays near London Bridge and had over twenty years' experience of the repair of the Bridge, an operation always dependent on the state of the tides.

Finally, there is Westminster Hall, which stands alone in size and in impressive dignity. Some description of this noble building has already been given, but nothing short of a whole volume would comprise a detailed analysis of its structure and beauties. Some allowance must be made for the Norman skeleton of the hall, but its massing as we see it is Yevele's, as is the whole of its main north front. It is unfortunate that its relative scale has been dwarfed by the building of the new Houses of Parliament, but even so its great length and the vast expanse of its roof are most impressive, as it crouches among the less dignified additions guarding the ancient regality of the palace of West-minster (23).

To sustain the thrusts of the great arched roof Yevele provided the western wall with six sturdy flying buttresses, which are surmounted by very finely proportioned pinnacles, square on plan, with gablets at the feet of the crowning pyramids. The peculiarly pleasant effect of these buttresses is due partly to the fact that they are of sufficient size to match the scale of the hall behind, but more to their being spaced out so that only one buttress occurs in each pair of bays. The full effect of the plain walling around the windows is thus maintained.

The entrance front is a most interesting and successful experiment in an unusual style of composition: the actual front gable of the hall with its great window is recessed between the two guardian towers, yet is saved from the usual weak appearance of recessed fronts by its grand proportions and by the monumental pinnacle at the apex, which contained in niches the statues of four Kings. Between the towers stands a noble porch on an intermediate plane between the gable and the front of the towers, whose faces up to the parapet of the porch are panelled with a canopy-work of niches and figures. Above this level are two storeys in the towers, which are finished off with embattled parapets. A particularly happy feature of the free-standing north-west tower is its stair-turret, which grows from the south-western angle of the tower in a most natural way, and relieves its plain surfaces of walling. The half-vaulting of the porch, like that at the west entrance of the Abbey, is so disposed that it seems to guide and welcome the visitor to the doors, a remarkable effect produced with the simplicity of so many effects of the great masters (23, 65).

Internally everything is contrived to emphasise the length and spaciousness of the vista; the plain lower walls are a foil for the roof, which springs from corbels of perfect proportions, themselves set in a carved string-course enriched with ever-varying versions of the White Hart badge. The rear-arches of the windows reflect the mouldings of the timber trusses and are kept far enough from the trusses to leave a solid abutment for the great arch, which satisfies the eye. The hood-moulds above the windows emphasise the correspondence between them and the arched trussing of the main purlins above, while the great south window poured a flood of light along the range of trefoil arches from end to end of the hall (41, 49).

Yevele's military architecture is less easy to discuss, because so little of it remains: Queenborough Castle has already been described; it was an isolated building of a type looking forward a century and more into the future, but it does not seem to have had any direct progeny (21, 22). It was begun in 1361, about the same time that the Bloody Tower and its vaulted gateway were being built at the Tower of London. This vault is irregular on plan, but the disposition of its ribs is similar to that which Yevele was employing at West-minster Abbey, with intermediate ribs between the transverse and diagonal arches, and between the latter and the wall. It cannot be said that the Bloody Tower has architectural claims equal to its historic interest, but the lions'

58 Westminster Abbey: Tomb of Edward III from the North-east. 1377

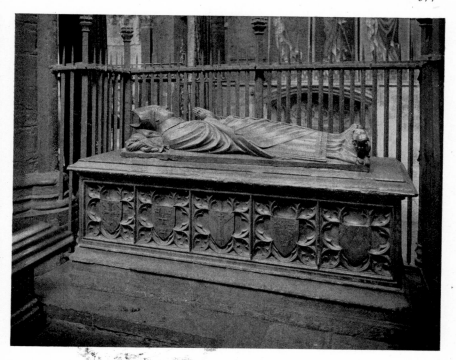

59 Westminster Abbey: Tomb of Cardinal Langham. *c.* 1389

61 London, Old St. Paul's: Tomb of Sir Simon Burley, K.G., c. 1389, from an engraving after Hollar. Note similarity of Tomb Chest to those of Edward III and Richard II, and of canopy to that of the tomb of Rahere.

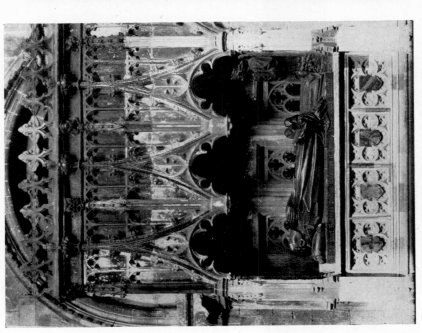

60 London, St. Bartholomew the Great: Tomb of Rahere from South. c. 1400

heads used for the corbels and bosses are matched in one of the contempory gateways in Windsor Castle. The relation of Wynford's work at Windsor to that of Yevele in London at this period would be most interesting to work out, for the precise degree of dependence of Windsor upon the London works establishment has never been determined.

There is a long interval before Yevele's next military works, undertaken in the national defence scare between 1378 and 1385. Though not attributed to him by direct documentary evidence, Yevele's responsibility for the West Gate at Canterbury seems certain. Here also are some striking resemblances to the "Norman" Gate to the Inner Ward at Windsor, built some fifteen years earlier. The Canterbury gate is a bigger and sturdier one, as befits its greater defensive importance. It is a most noble and impressive work, with a narrow but well-proportioned archway within a square frame between its two great drum-towers. The drums stand on a projecting plinth, and between the plinth and the parapet their height is bisected by a string-course, the upper stage being slightly set back (26, 32). The median string-course continues across the wall above the archway, but is saved from appearing to cut the gate in half by the embattled parapets of the towers, and by the placing of the machicolated parapet above the gateway on a lower level. There are no windows in the drum-towers, and the loups are hardly visible at a slight distance, so that the powerful architectonic effect of the gatehouse lies entirely in its composition. On the inner face of the gateway is a two-light window, with a traceried head of precisely the same detail as Yevele's windows in the new Westminster Hall (27).

The Thames defence towers of 1380 were either never built, or soon disappeared, but there are still considerable remains of Lord Cobham's castle at Cowling in Kent, built within the next four years. The gatehouse is intact, and is very similar to the Canterbury West Gate; the castle was square in plan, and deserves careful comparison with Bodiam, begun in 1385, and which may also have been designed by Yevele (38, 62, 63).

Quite definitely in Yevele's style, and even more closely akin to the Canterbury gate, is the great keep-gatehouse of Archbishop Courtenay's castle of Saltwood, near Hythe (37, 39). This is a magnificent gatehouse of great height, worthy of comparison with the original Dunstanburgh gatehouse of 1314. It was probably built during the 1380's, while work under Yevele was still in progress on the walls of Canterbury. Yevele's last military works, at the castles of Winchester and Canterbury, consisted only of repairs, and little or nothing has remained to the present day.

Finally, most important of all his works, are his essays in church architecture and in monuments, forms which invite some comparison with absolute music, freed as they are from directly utilitarian considerations. Disregarding such doubtful early works as the additions to St. Katherine's-by-the-Tower, Yevele's first work in this class is the west cloister of Westminster Abbey, with the planning of the new nave (8, 56). The pierced arcading of the cloister takes the form of four-light windows with reticulated heads of the "straight" Perpendicular type, the reticulations being filled with beautiful foliations.

Between the arches are simple buttresses with one splayed offset above the springing level. Apart from a moulded plinth which runs below the windows and continues round the buttresses, and a coping, this is the whole of the cloister's external elevation. The vaults have ridge-ribs and one pair of tiercerons, or intermediate ribs, in each direction, and carved bosses. There are also two very beautiful examples of blind spandrel tracery, over the doorway leading into the nave, and over a recess in the bay next to the south-

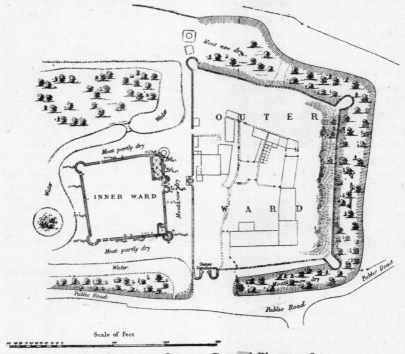

62. COWLING CASTLE: Ground Plan. 1380.

west corner; the patterns used are geometric in character, though there is a hint of the Flamboyant in two pierced "wheels" above the nave door.

The nave of the abbey church is one of Yevele's biggest works, and is certainly a most brilliant example of adaptation to a pre-existing design. The whole elevation was controlled by the lines of the thirteenth-century bays of the choir, but the detail of the new work, mouldings, bases and caps, is all Yevele's. The old piers had detached marble shafts, but the new ones were built in the solid, with eight rounded shafts growing out of the central core. The bands, which on the original work held the lengths of marble shafting in position, were reproduced for purely aesthetic reasons, to match the old work (55). It was only in the design for the west front that Yevele was able to give his originality free play. Internally, the door and great window were made to form parts of a unified scheme of tracery covering the whole wall. The window of seven lights was divided by two main mullions on each side of the three-light centrepiece, and these mullions were continued downwards, enclosing the door beneath, while the subsidiary mullions were also carried down to a plinth. This internal tracery design is almost exactly paralleled at the west end of Canterbury nave, and the Canterbury porch also closely follows the Westminster design (64, 65).

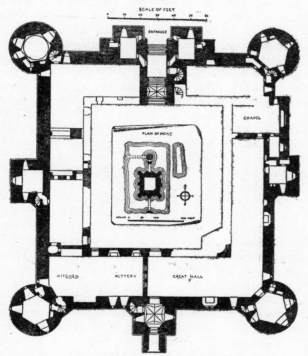

63. BODIAM CASTLE: Ground Plan. 1385.

Externally, the Westminster front is as wide as the overall width of the nave and its buttresses, the lateral towers being provided with great clasping buttresses at the angles, carried vertically upwards, an unusual feature rather similar to certain church towers of Bedfordshire and Northamptonshire. There is an even closer resemblance to the scheme of the western towers of St. Gudule at Brussels, also begun towards the end of the fourteenth century. It is by no means impossible that Yevele and the Brabant master may have been in communication with each other, in view of the close relations then subsisting between England and the Low Countries.

The wide faces of the Abbey buttresses are enriched with vertical strips and tracery, with canopies above each stage; the two interior buttresses on

10

each side of the west window have each a beautiful addition in the form of a narrower projecting buttress, dying back by stages into the main face. These subsidiary buttresses contain the porch and its superimposed screen-work of canopied niches. Owing to the stoppage of work at the Dissolution Yevele's intentions as to the upper part of the towers were never carried out, and his design is unknown. What remains is a grandly strong façade, bounded by an exact square of just over 100 feet from side to side, and from the ground to the string course above the great window. This may well have been intentional, for the west front of Notre Dame at Paris also forms an exact square (36).

Yevele must have been designing the new work at the Abbey soon after 1360, and by about 1363 he was probably engaged on the transformation of part of the crypt of Canterbury Cathedral into a chantry chapel for his patron the Black Prince. This was beneath the south-east transept of the cathedral, and consisted on plan of four bays disposed in a square about a central pier, while deeply recessed windows to the East took the place of the Norman apses. The lierne vaulting is elaborate, and anticipates one curious feature of the high vault of the nave, namely the use of lierne ribs springing from the curve of the wall- and cross-arches, to the ridges. The hand of a collaborator, probably John Box, is to be seen in the window tracery, and very likely in other details (17, 67).

The simple western tower of Cobham Church in Kent, built about 1370, is not unlike Yevele's Westminster clock-tower, and belongs to his school, if it is not by his own hand. Some ten years later the important collegiate church of Arundel contains details which were probably either designed by him or closely imitated from his work. Similar details are found at Westbourne Church, Sussex, and elsewhere on the Arundel estates, as far away as Brockenhurst in Hampshire.[1]

Very little architectural detail remains from Yevele's work of 1371 at the London Charterhouse (30), and his next extant work is the first period of the nave at Canterbury, apparently comprising the side-walls of the aisles, built between 1377 and 1381. The windows are somewhat unusual in design, having four lights made up by putting together two two-light windows with traceried transoms and reticulated heads, and filling up the spandrel beneath the head of the main arch with a smaller version of the two-light pattern in the centre, and vertical panels at the sides. The single reticulations of the lower two-light sections have straight sides and internal foliation, this resembling the work in the Westminster cloister. Beneath the sill the mullions are carried downwards for an additional blind stage, with traceried heads below the sill, like those under the transom in the window. Altogether these are satisfying windows, for they have much of the richness of Decorated tracery, coupled with the increased verticality of the new style. The Canterbury aisles are in fact extremely high, a feature no doubt borrowed from the thirteenth-century precedent at Westminster (55, 66).

Although there was an interval of some ten years before work was resumed

[1] Sussex Archæol. Coll. XXII, 1870, p. 81.

64 Canterbury Cathedral: West Porch. *c.* 1391

65 Westminster Abbey: West Porch, 1362 and later;
The niches above the porch were carried out after
Yevele's death, with altered detail

66 Canterbury Cathedral: the Nave looking East. 1377; 1391

at Canterbury, the design must be considered as a whole at this stage, for it must have been substantially complete when the aisles were begun. In many details, and as a whole, the nave of Canterbury is the very finest product of English Gothic. The magnificent compound piers give assurance of stability, and the triple shafts which carry the high vault lead the eye upwards to the lierne tracery above. The vaulting itself is more perfectly proportioned and poised than any other extant example: the ribs grow with lovely sweeping curves from the shafts, the great diagonals being kept back so that they do not break the pure line of the swelling sheaf as it bursts outwards into the void. The tiercerons are beautifully subordinated to the main ribs, as though they

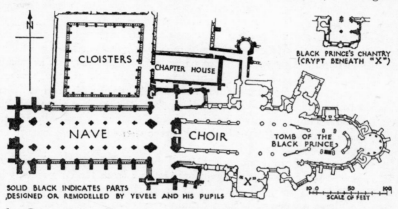

67. CANTERBURY CATHEDRAL: Plan to show work designed 1363–1400.

were parts of some natural growth, and the liernes form a four-petalled flower around each intersection of the main diagonals. The bosses have been criticised as too small for the scale of the building, but besides permitting the great sweep of the diagonals to be seen, this smallness of the bosses has the more subtle effect of increasing the apparent height of the vault, a gain which to me seems more than to counterbalance any lack of scale in the bosses themselves. Again, it is said that the clerestory windows are too small, but in fact the dimmer lighting of the high vault, contrasting with the flood of light from the tall aisle windows, also adds to the apparent height and lends a needed touch of mystery to the vaulting.

The rings breaking the rise of the vertical shafts have been much criticised; they are certainly reminiscent of the annulets at Westminster and were doubtless suggested by the use of such rings there and at many other buildings, as for example on the crossing piers of Lichfield Cathedral, but at Canterbury they were probably inserted with the idea of breaking the monotony of a very long continuous line, and their use seems to have been justified. One of the most brilliant features of the whole composition is the horizontal link provided by the mouldings above the main arcades, and the transom in the blind tracery at the sill of the clerestory windows; by this means the unity of the whole nave is suggested without any interruption of the vertical lines of the piers. Altogether, the nave of Canterbury is the finest interior now remaining in England, and one of the greatest masterpieces of art in the world.

Of other ecclesiastical work designed by Yevele little is known: only the outer arch of his east window at Battersea survives, and nothing of his aisle and porch at St. Dunstan's in the East. The spacious church at Maidstone, with its simple and grandly proportioned tower certainly owes something to him, but it can hardly have been designed as a whole by Yevele in person; perhaps it may prove to be the work of Stephen Lote, following Yevele's sketches, like the cloister and chapter-house at Canterbury. On the other hand, Archbishop Courtenay's additions to Meopham Church may have been carried out under Yevele, but evidence is lacking.

Yevele's monumental work is of considerable importance, and bulked largely in his output, while he certainly must have designed a large number of monuments now destroyed, and of which no record exists. The tomb of Sir John Beauchamp, K.G., in old St. Paul's, made about 1360, was quite probably designed by Yevele, for not only did he make a bequest in his will for masses to be said for the soul of Sir John Beauchamp, but the tomb-chest shown in Hollar's engraving, with panelled sides formed of cusped quatrefoils holding shields, might well have been the forerunner of Yevele's mature type, seen in the tomb of Edward III (50).

His canopied tomb of about 1374 for John of Gaunt and the Duchess Blanche, also in old St. Paul's, is again only known from Hollar's view, which shows that it had a recessed centre and projecting open-work "towers" at each end. These towers with their canopy-work had a considerable likeness to the four-square design of the west front of Westminster Abbey, the open-work of the tomb-canopy representing the blind tracery on the great buttresses of the Abbey towers. The tomb itself, which was made of alabaster from Yevele's own district, had canopies along its sides, apparently more definitely transitional in style than those of the tomb of Edward III (51).

This latter tomb is the finest of the series, and its description will serve, with certain slight modifications, for all the rest. Owing to the difference in level between the aisle and the Confessor's Chapel in Westminster Abbey, the actual tomb rests on a panelled sub-base on one side only. The sub-base comprises four square panels, each filled with a cusped quatrefoil holding a shield, while the corners between the foils are occupied by vesica-shaped petals, with internal ogee cusping. The sides of the tomb have six niches, each surmounted by a projecting canopy of three gablets, while beneath the figures of weepers in the niches are small square panels, with quatrefoils containing shields. Between each pair of niches is two-light blind tracery, with ogee canopies level with those above the niches (28, 58).

The tomb of Richard II and Anne of Bohemia has eight niches instead of six, and five square panels in the sub-base (53); that of Cardinal Langham has the pattern of the sub-base only, resting on a moulded plinth: in this instance also there are five square panels (59). The Black Prince's tomb in Canterbury Cathedral has the same general arrangement as Langham's, but there are six panels, rather taller than squares, containing cusped eight-foils holding shields; the pattern of these cusped panels is also found outside the west porch of Canterbury, and in a similar position on Yevele's west porch of Westminster Abbey. Along the plinth is a row of 29 small squares, each with a diagonal quatrefoil (18).

Two other tombs which may well have been designed by Yevele were those for Sir Walter Manny in the Chapel of the London Charterhouse, and for Sir Simon Burley in St. Paul's Cathedral. Manny's will, made shortly before his death in the winter of 1371-72, directed that "a tomb of alabaster with my image as a knight and my arms thereon shall be made for me like unto that of Sir John Beauchamp in St. Paul's in London." The extant fragment (31), part of a niche-head and "buttress," suggests that the tomb's sides were recessed for weepers. The work was delicately painted and gilt, and the arch is provided with cusping exactly similar to that of the doorways through the Durham Neville Screen, shortly to be discussed.

Burley's tomb, probably made after the overthrow of the Appellants in 1389, had an elaborate canopy similar to the wooden tester over Edward III's tomb at Westminster, and to the canopy of Rahere's tomb in St. Bartholomew's, Smithfield. To be classed with these canopies are the sedilia of c. 1370 in the chancel at Cobham, Kent, and the lovely stone pulpit in the nave of Arundel Church. The tomb of 1374 for the Earl and Countess of Arundel may be represented by that in the north nave aisle of Chichester Cathedral, which though modern preserves a design much like that of the tomb of Sir John Beauchamp in St. Paul's. Of the same type is the tomb of Sir William Marney, who died in 1360, at Layer Marney in Essex.

Rahere's tomb in the priory church of St. Bartholomew the Great, is similar to that of Langham, but with only four square panels along the side; instead of standing free it is enclosed in a vaulted canopy of stone. This consists of three bays, with an additional blind bay to the east of the tomb itself, while two more bays, now destroyed, enclosed a chantry chamber entered from the presbytery by a door. Each bay consists of a cinquefoliated cusped arch, surmounted by a crocketed canopy, behind which is blind tracery; above is a cornice and cresting. The blind walling towards the ambulatory is pierced by square-headed windows, each containing an arched two-light of Yevele's favourite design, like the side windows of Westminster Hall. The whole tomb is most beautifully executed, an especially charming feature being the pairs of little buttresses, splayed diagonally towards the sanctuary, at the ends, and on the "pier" between the tomb and the blind bay (60).

Finally, though it is only a presumed work of Yevele, mention must be made of the splendid Neville Screen or reredos in Durham Cathedral. The screen consists of five tall spires of openwork, separated by four shorter spires; each spire is flanked by a diagonal buttress, which is itself supported by two diagonal buttresses, in similar fashion to those on Rahere's tomb. The lowest storey of the screen contains side doorways, and forms the reredos to the High Altar; above this is a series of niches for life-size statues, with pedestals.

crowned by canopies of three gablets supported by double-cusped arches. The shorter spires have narrower niches with canopies of two gablets, and an open-work spire above; the five tall spires interpose another storey of canopied niches above the first. The strong vertical emphasis of the sets of double buttresses, which themselves occur in pairs between the spires, and the firm horizontal bond above the bottom storey give cohesion to the whole, and make it a most remarkable composition. It contains many details and motives typical of Yevele, and must almost certainly have been designed by him: if so, it is his masterpiece in the realms of pure art and ornament (33, 34).

ADDENDA TO SECOND EDITION

THE FAMILY OF "YEAVELEY" CAN BE TRACED BACK TO THE TWELFTH CENTURY. RALPH "DE Giuelega" appears at Barton Blount (4 miles from Yeaveley) before 1167; in 1278 John "le Mazon de Iueleg' ", and in 1281 Matthew "de Yueley" occur in the Assizes for Derbyshire as pledges of suitors in cases concerning common rights in other neighbouring parishes. This proves the free status of the family, and also that at least one mason was to be found at Yeaveley in the late thirteenth century. (Jeayes: *Derbyshire Charters*, No. 238; P.R.O. Assize Rolls, 1238, m. 25d; 147, m. 5, communicated by Mr. C. E. Lugard).

Henry Yevele was twice concerned with work for St. Albans Abbey during the abbacy of Thomas de la Mare (1349–96). On the first occasion the townsmen encroached upon the wall running from the west end of the church to Holywell Gate, and a survey was made by the Abbot's steward John of Middleton and "Master Henry Zevelee of London, mason." When walls were built from the King's Hall to the Almonry, the work was under the control of a lay-brother William Stubarde, together with John Bukkedene and John Clifford, deputies (*substituti*) of Master Henry Zevele. (*Gesta Abbatum*, Rolls Ser., iii, 186, 387; I am indebted to Mr. Arthur Oswald for this reference). It is worth noting that the Great Gatehouse at St. Albans was built about 1362–65, and that its cresting was replaced with Kentish ragstone between 1396 and 1401.

In 1383–4 one of Yevele's properties in Basing Lane was being rented by John of Gaunt, who paid (*in redditu solut. Henr. de zeweley pro vno hospic . . . in Basynglane*) at the rate of £3 6s. 8d. a year. (M. R. James: *Catalogue of MSS. of Peterhouse*, 1899, 61; *Bulletin of Inst. Hist. Research*, XIII, 154–60).

In 1388–9 "Yveley", in company with "Wm. Wynford" and "Herland", and their "families" (probably assistants), dined in Hall with the Fellows of New College, Oxford. Wynford and Herland also dined there together on one occasion, and Wynford alone on a second, in 1390–91. (Hall books of New College, communicated by Professor John L. Myres, Librarian).

Among the archives of Canterbury Cathedral an account of Prior Chillenden for 1396–7 shows that 20 masons (*latomi*), 3 setters (*leggeres*), and 4 workmen were then at work on the church, while £90 16s. was paid to "Master Henry Ivele" for lead and stone bought from him. These may have been surplus stores from the official work on the castle and city walls, then in his charge. (Prior's Account Roll, xvii. 4, communicated by Mr. W. P. Blore, Chapter Librarian).

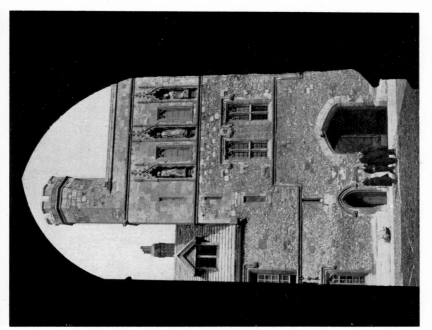

69 Winchester College: Gatehouse. 1388
Designer: William Wynford

68 Winchester College: Chapel, interior looking East. 1388
Designer: William Wynford; (of vault) Hugh Herland

71 Winchester Cathedral: West Front. *c.* 1360. Parapets and gable added, *c.* 1395, by William Wynford

70 Winchester Cathedral: Nave, looking West. 1394 Designer: William Wynford

Chapter VI

Contemporaries and Successors

GREAT AS YEVELE WAS, HE WAS NO ISOLATED PHENOMENON; HIS whole period is thronged with architects of the first rank, and there must have been fruitful exchanges of ideas between most of these remarkable men. Next to Yevele in importance was William Wynford, a master mason whose career was parallel to Yevele's, though Wynford must have been a few years the younger. He probably came from Winford in Somerset, a small village some six miles south-west of Bristol; his early life and Yevele's must have been subject to similar influences, but instead of settling in London, he obtained employment on the King's works at Windsor Castle, where he was warden of the mason's work under John Sponlee by 1360, and joint disposer of the work with Sponlee in the following year. William of Wykeham was clerk of the works at Windsor from 1356 to the end of 1361, and Wynford appears as Wykeham's architect for more than forty years afterwards. Whatever the origin of their acquaintanceship may have been, there is no doubt as to the close relation of the master craftsman to the building enterprises of the great cleric and prelate.

Wykeham became provost of Wells Cathedral in 1363, and Wynford became consultant master mason there a year later; meanwhile he continued to be one of the masters in charge at Windsor, and from about 1365 he seems to have taken responsibility from Sponlee, who was granted a corrody at Reading Abbey. Wynford obtained from the King a life-pension of £10 a year in 1372, and from that time onwards spent a large proportion of his time on private practice. In 1375 he was master mason to Abingdon Abbey, while a year or so later he was in charge of repair work at Corfe Castle for the Crown. Wynford was almost certainly the architect for Wykeham's New College at Oxford, begun in 1380, and was definitely the designer of Winchester College, built between 1388 and 1394. As has been seen already, Wynford appeared as a colleague of Yevele on the commissions for repairing Winchester Castle in 1390 and 1397, and in 1394 he was in charge of work at Highclere, one of Wykeham's episcopal manor-houses in Hampshire. At Winchester College, Wynford's portrait was included in the east window of the chapel, beside those of Simon Membury, the clerk of works, and the carpenter, who was almost certainly Hugh Herland (48, 68, 69).

After the completion of the College, Wynford proceeded with the reconstruction of Winchester Cathedral in Perpendicular style; he preserved the core of the old Norman nave without demolition, and this resulted in a work of extremely sturdy character, though not quite so beautifully proportioned in its parts as the work of Yevele at Canterbury (70, 71). The nave of Winchester is nevertheless one of the supreme triumphs of English Gothic, and marks Wynford as a great ecclesiastical architect second only to Yevele, while the royal lodgings at Windsor and his two colleges show him to have been also a master of domestic planning. Another brilliant example of Wynford's powers is the south-west tower of Wells Cathedral, which he was able to add to the early thirteenth-century front without incongruity, and with most happy results. The north-west tower, though executed with slight changes of detail after his death, evidently completes his scheme, which makes Wells the most satisfying English cathedral front in existence.

Another architect of great importance was John Clyve, the master mason of Worcester Cathedral during the generation following 1360. He completed the nave and built the west front, the north porch, and the cloister, but his principal achievement was the splendid central tower, from which the later towers of Gloucester Abbey, Malvern Priory, and many others were derived. This tower is not only of importance for its own sake, supremely beautiful as it is, but because it is the only central tower of first-class design and scale which survives from its period. It is thus the first great tower of the Perpendicular style, and shows interesting borrowings from its late Decorated predecessors at Wells and Salisbury (15).

Away in the north was yet another great architect, practising in an even barer and sterner style than Yevele's own. This was John Lewyn, the chief mason to the Palatine Bishop of Durham, and to the Prior and Chapter of Durham Cathedral. Lewyn was responsible for most of the important works in the northern counties built between 1360 and 1400. Besides the remarkable vaulted kitchen at Durham, he carried out extensive works at the castles of Bamburgh, Dunstanburgh, Carlisle, and Roxburgh, and built Bolton Castle in Wensleydale. The new keep of Durham Castle and the great donjon of Warkworth were probably also designed by him. Lewyn had at least one contact with the leaders of the London school, when in 1380 he erected in Durham Cathedral the great Neville Screen or reredos, which had been made in London, probably to Yevele's design, of clunch or hard chalk, and shipped to Durham by way of Newcastle-on-Tyne.

Two other provincial contemporaries of Yevele produced works of first-class importance: Robert Skillington who built John of Gaunt's great hall and state apartments at Kenilworth Castle during the 1380's and '90's; and John Meppushal, who after working at Cambridge in the '70's became master mason of Ely Minster and produced the magnificent "Porta" or great gatehouse, and the octagonal lantern of the Minster's west tower.

Characteristic of Yevele's school is the employment of large expanses of plain walling, so marked at Kenilworth and the Ely Gatehouse, at Wynford's Colleges and Lewyn's Castles. These architects could all employ enrichment internally, but never lost their sense of proportion, and when the enrichment spread to the exterior, as it did in Clyve's work at Worcester, it was not permitted to overstep the limits of its usefulness, as was to happen so often with the panelling of the fifteenth and sixteenth centuries.

These men were Yevele's greatest rivals in his own craft, but greater than any of them was the carpenter Hugh Herland, whose position in architectural history is as high as Yevele's own. Herland sprang from a family which had been at the head of the King's carpentry works for two generations before his time. He therefore not only inherited a genius for the craft, but was surrounded by the massed traditions of England's finest timberwork. Comparatively little of Herland's known work has survived, but from simple roofs such as that of the Abbot's new hall at Westminster he progressed to his great masterpiece, the roof of Westminster Hall, built between 1394 and 1400. This marvellous roof is quite without a rival in any part of the world, not only for the ingenuity of its construction, but on account of the perfection and delicacy of its details, which recall Herland's earlier work, the little tester over the tomb of Edward III in the Abbey (41, 58).

Another roof which must be attributed to Hugh Herland is the wooden vault of the chapel at Winchester College. This is notable for its anticipation of large-scale fan-tracery, though its "fans" are unusual in forming pointed arches, not semicircles, on plan, and are thus exceptionally well fitted for covering a Gothic chapel (68). Unfortunately the idea was never developed by the masons, who adopted the easier but less lovely conoids of the true fan-vault.

Except for Lewyn, who died about 1398, most if not all of these men survived Yevele, but by 1400 they were already in old age, and the carrying on of Yevele's principles was left to a younger generation of men who had been his junior partners in the last twenty years of his life. Something has already been said of these younger men, who carried a part of Yevele's spirit into the sad and desolate years of the early fifteenth century, a time when the pulse of English art almost stopped. Four chief disciples are worthy of special mention: John Clifford, William Colchester, Stephen Lote, and Walter Walton. Clifford worked at Windsor Castle in the 1360's, but later settled in London, and by 1386 had become chief mason of London Bridge, a post which he may have owed to Yevele, who as one of the Bridge Wardens was in a position of control there. Clifford acted in association with Yevele in connection with the work and administration of the Bridge, and doubtless passed on to Richard Beke, his deputy and successor, some of Yevele's skill as a bridge-builder. Westminster Abbey was the section of the old master's work which fell to Colchester's share, and he faithfully continued Yevele's design for the nave and west front there. In 1407 he was, however, sent to York Minster by the King to take charge of the work of the central tower, where a collapse had occurred. As a "foreigner" he at first encountered great opposition among the York masons, some of whom joined in a conspiracy which resulted in severe injuries to Colchester and to his assistant, who nearly died of his wounds. In 1416 Colchester became a freeman of York, and it is to be presumed that he must by that time have overcome local prejudices. His noble tower was at any rate recognised as one of the crowning glories of the Minster, and remains as his only known work of importance. He became master mason to the King in 1418, on the death of Stephen Lote, but only lived to enjoy the office for two years, a period occupied by Henry V's second French campaign.

Stephen Lote was a man of Kent, and may well have been working at Canterbury when he first met Yevele. He first appears in the early 1390's, working for the Queen, Anne of Bohemia, and for John of Gaunt, as well as helping Yevele to make the tombs of Cardinal Langham and the King and Queen in Westminster Abbey (53, 59). Like Yevele, he owned property at Wennington in Essex, and he certainly acted as deputy to Yevele at Canterbury Cathedral, and succeeded him as master of the new works there in 1400. With Clifford, he was an executor of Yevele's will, and as his successor in the office of King's Mason must have inherited most of Yevele's craft traditions. In addition to the completion of the nave, cloisters, and chapter-house at Canterbury, Lote worked at Shene Palace (25) and at the collegiate church of Fotheringhay, Northants., as well as visiting Rochester Bridge as consultant architect.

Lote was a close friend of Walter Walton, the remaining member of this quadrumvirate. Walton was a London mason, who had rebuilt the church of the Hospital of St. Thomas of Acon in 1383, and later became warden or deputy to Yevele at Westminster Hall. In 1397 he received a special appointment as chief surveyor of the masons employed on the King's works, and after Yevele's death he worked at Shene Palace (25) in close association with Lote, and also ran a private practice in the city; in 1412 he and his wife Joan owned Seymores Manor in Blo Norton in Norfolk, ten miles east of Thetford.[1]

Another mason who came into personal contact with Yevele in his last years was Thomas Wolvey of St. Albans, who worked at Westminster Hall and was also the builder of a great part of the church of Henley-on-Thames in Oxfordshire. Wolvey died in 1428, but he was succeeded in his craft by a son John, who died in 1462, and the latter's son Richard, who died at the end of 1493, when the line seems to have died out. It is quite probable that the Wolveys were masons to St. Albans Abbey, in which case they would have had opportunities for exercising a wide influence on the architecture of western Hertfordshire, and other places connected with the great abbey. Thomas Wolvey, as has been seen, very probably designed the St. Albans clock-tower in imitation of Yevele's at Westminster.

The generation which had worked with Yevele was dying out by 1420, and its place was taken by a number of younger men who only touched the tradition at second hand. Chief among these were Thomas Mapilton and John Thirsk. Mapilton was the son of a London mason and marbler, but had been master mason at Durham Cathedral from 1408 to 1416. He then returned to London and shortly afterwards continued Lote's work for the Duke of York at Fotheringhay. Mapilton also entered the service of the Crown, and went abroad in the train of Henry V in 1418; on the conclusion of peace in 1420 it seems probable that he went on to Florence as one of a number of foreign architects who were invited by the Florentines to advise on the roofing of the central space of S. Maria del Fiore. Though the great

[1] W. Rye, Norfolk Feet of Fines, II, 401.

Italian master, Filippo Brunelleschi, was ultimately the chosen designer, the fact of having been invited to travel to such a renowned city as Florence would have been a great addition to the prestige of a fifteenth century London architect. By the summer of 1421 Mapilton had succeeded William Colchester as the King's Master Mason, and he also became consultant architect to Rochester Bridge and Canterbury Cathedral, where he designed the south-west tower. This tower, now matched by a modern copy on the north side of the nave, is an important work, for it set a fashion followed by many smaller towers in Kent and elsewhere. Its detail and proportions are by no means so satisfactory as those of Yevele's work alongside, but the general composition is good, and the unusual pinnacles are markedly successful. Mapilton acquired a great reputation, and was called in by Bury St. Edmunds Abbey to try to save the great west tower of the church, which was, however, too far gone for anything to be done. In 1435, three years before his death, Mapilton joined the London Skinners' Fraternity of Our Lady of the Assumption, in company with John Thirsk, the Westminster Abbey mason. Thirsk was a Yorkshireman, and he doubtless owed his position at Westminster to William Colchester, with whom he must have worked at York Minster. After Colchester's death in 1420, Thirsk continued the rebuilding of the Abbey nave, and began the fine Chantry Chapel of Henry V, a work which adapted much of Yevele's traditional detail. Thirsk also designed the great reredos, whose eastern face still remains, though in a damaged condition. Thirsk came into personal contact with Henry VI, when that King was choosing a position for his tomb, which, however, was never built in the Abbey owing to the civil war. To this meeting Thirsk probably owed his appointment in 1449 as master mason of Windsor Castle, an office which he held until his death three years later.

Meanwhile, Richard Beke the London Bridge mason, who had worked under John Clifford, had taken Mapilton's place at Canterbury Cathedral, and continued in charge there from 1435 until his death in 1458. At Canterbury Beke seems to have "snatched" an office which was almost within the grasp of Thomas Stanley, who had been the senior working mason there in Mapilton's time. Stanley had already been promoted to the rank of an esquire among the Prior's servants in 1432, when Beke first appeared at Canterbury as a consultant, owing to Mapilton's absorption in London business. After losing the chance of becoming architect to the Cathedral, Stanley left its employ altogether and built up a practice as contractor for parochial works, such as the church towers at Lydd, built by him between 1442 and 1446, and Tenterden. These towers are modelled on Mapilton's south-west tower at Canterbury, and their simplicity and strength are clearly derived from the influence of Yevele, which still gave a certain confident direction to the architecture of south-east England.

Canterbury had gathered to itself a great part of the best talent during the years of architectural depression which had followed the Lancastrian usurpation, and when Henry VI founded Eton College, it was to Canterbury that his architect, Robert Westerley, went for many of his craftsmen.

Westerley himself may have come from Westerleigh in Gloucestershire, but he was in the royal service for many years before Mapilton's death, and must have absorbed the traditions of the London school. But other western masons were coming into prominence, notably the Janyns family, who seem to have been Oxford men. The accession of Edward IV in 1461 had the unfortunate effect of putting a stop to the great building projects of Henry VI, which had already been slowed by the political crisis, and King Edward also found it necessary to remove most of the chief craftsmen from their offices, replacing them by men who may well have been loyal Yorkists, but are hardly likely to have been so imbued with the old traditions as the men they superseded. The new mason, Thomas Jurden, had, as a matter of fact, worked for a couple of years at Eton, and was already chief mason of London Bridge; by the time that Edward IV was beginning to indulge in architectural pursuits, about 1475, Jurdan was able to design for him the fine hall of Eltham Palace, one of the noblest apartments in the royal dwellings.

Work was also begun on St. George's Chapel in Windsor Castle in 1475, and there the chosen architect was Henry Janyns, who had served part of his apprenticeship at Eton, and was the son of Robert Janyns, the designer of the bell-tower of Merton College, Oxford, and later warden of the masons at Eton College. The Janyns dynasty was continued by a second Robert, probably son of Henry; this younger Robert became master mason of Windsor Castle in Henry VII's time, and was associated with Robert Vertue as one of the King's Master Masons.

Other lines of "descent" from Yevele, by pupilage and contact, were to be found at Westminster Abbey and Canterbury. John Smyth, who had worked under Mapilton and Beke at Canterbury, became warden of the masons at Eton in 1441, under Westerley, and in 1452 succeeded Thirsk as master mason to Westminster Abbey. Thomas Glasier, another of the Eton masons, was granted the office of mason to Canterbury Cathedral after Beke's death in 1458, and Robert Stowell, who had become master at Windsor Castle on Thirsk's death in 1452, though he lost this appointment after Edward IV's accession, ultimately became master at Westminster Abbey, a post which he held from 1471 to 1505.

It is impossible to follow these contacts further in a brief space, and attention must be transferred to the last great masters of the Gothic age: John Wastell, the brothers Robert and William Vertue, and Henry Redman. Wastell was perhaps trained at Canterbury; at any rate his first known work is the completion of the great central tower of the Cathedral, the Angel Steeple or Bell Harry. A new central tower must have been contemplated by Yevele and Lote, and definite steps were taken by Beke to strengthen the crossing piers for the load, but the tower was not carried beyond the ridges of the great roofs until 1490, when Wastell began the external tower and the beautiful openwork screens which buttress the piers beneath. After finishing this tower about 1497, Wastell moved to Bury St. Edmunds, where he seems to have worked for the Abbey, and which remained his home for the rest of his life. He was called as far afield as Peterborough, where he designed the eastern ambulatory chapels, and to Cambridge, to build the great vaults of King's College Chapel. The grand sweeping lines of Wastell's work derive from the old tradition of Yevele and the London school, but to this was added an incrustation of carved detail, almost of filigree character, which unfortunately began to distract the eye from purity of line and composition to meretricious surface enrichments, albeit produced with great skill and the most extravagant craftsmanship.

The Vertues also seem to have come from Canterbury, for when Robert made his will in 1506 he desired to be buried in the Abbey of St. Augustine there. A close similarity exists between the styles of Wastell and the Vertues, though they can easily be distinguished from each other. Robert Vertue died in 1506, but William lived until 1527, and completed works which had been begun by his brother, so that William bulks larger in history, though they should strictly be considered together, like the Adam brothers. Their greatest works are the new church of Bath Abbey, the vaults of St. George's Chapel, Windsor, and above all the amazing chapel of Henry VII at Westminster Abbey. This last is a *coup de maître* of sheer mason-craft, inspired with lovely pattern-work and carving of the most delicate description. The constructional skill displayed has its roots in the past, but the ornament is too lavish and gives a somewhat "Rococo" impression. Gothic art badly needed rescue from this tendency to over-elaboration, and the rescuer was waiting his opportunity, in the person of Henry Redman.

Redman was the son of Thomas Redman, master mason of Westminster Abbey, and his family came from Huntingdonshire, not far from Ramsey, where the great abbey may have been their ultimate artistic source. Henry Redman was a close friend and associate of William Vertue, but while he shared with Vertue the office of King's Master Mason, his real chances came from outside the royal service. He had genius for large-scale domestic work, which he first displayed at Eton College, where the west side of the court and Lupton's Tower were built to his designs. When Wolsey became Archbishop of York in 1514 he engaged Redman as architect for his vast building schemes, and in the next ten years Redman built Wolsey's Hampton Court, then the new hall and other works at York Place (Whitehall Palace), and finally Cardinal College (now Christ Church), Oxford, which was still in progress at the time of Redman's death in 1528. His grasp of the essentials of architecture was immense, and unlike Vertue and most of his contemporaries, he was well able to subordinate detail to the general composition, and revived Yevele's scheme of setting off windows and turrets with great expanses of plain walling. Had Redman lived a few years longer, he might have produced a new style strong enough to resist the novelty of the Renaissance. Unfortunately for English architecture, Redman died at the height of his career, and the vital impetus of the Tudor style died with him. Much of the old tradition persisted in the work of his successor John Molton, as at St. James's Palace and Henry VIII's additions to Hampton Court, but the style was already debased and mingled with foreign detail long before the deaths of Molton and the King in 1547.

One other architect of this final period deserves special mention, for he too might have saved Gothic architecture, by giving it a "modernist" or "functionalist" trend. This was Christopher Scune or Scoign, architect for the completion of the steeple of Louth Church, Lincs., from 1506 to 1515, and designer of the new nave and tower of Ripon Minster, built between 1503 and 1521. The Louth spire is by general consent one of the very finest ever built, but the Perpendicular work at Ripon has been curiously over-looked. It is intensely vital and shows distinct signs of breaking away from the stock forms of the period. Particularly fine are the great piers and arches of the east and south sides of the crossing, standing in aloof magnificence beside the old arches of the north and west sides, which were never replaced. The roll mouldings of the new piers follow a continuous curve on plan, having no fillets whatever. This contributes to their effect of growth and vitality, and it is difficult to picture them having been built stone by stone. The sharply pointed arches, too, follow an unusual curve, and seem to pierce the future as well as the heights of the lantern. Such forms, centuries later, were to commend themselves to architects working in reinforced concrete, and striving after the inexpressible.

With Redman and Scune died the last hope of a new Gothic style for England, a style founded in the past, yet truly living, and adapted to actual needs. The disruptive results of artistic dictation by the dead hand of classic Rome soon became apparent, and architectural invention tended to disappear, giving place to the monotonous game of piecing together bits of the classic orders in new ways, an occupation worthy of some mechanical contrivance designed in the Academy of Lagado, rather than of the human brain. The Roman Renaissance imposed a terrible handicap on architectural genius, hardly to be surmounted even by a Wren, but regret for past mistakes is useless; only the production of a genuine national architecture could be accepted as a proof of "true repentance," and for such a proof it is never too late.

In following the traces of Yevele's influence during the hundred and fifty years following his death, Yevele himself has been somewhat neglected. By the great world he always has been neglected, even when allowance has been made for the fact that Architecture is the art least recognised by the general public. It is difficult to see why architecture should receive so little attention, for it is, like music, expressed in an universal language, and the Old World, and especially England, is well equipped with good examples ranging over a period of many centuries. But even though architecture has now received a certain amount of public recognition in this country, there are probably few laymen who could name even three or four English architects earlier than Inigo Jones. This book attempts to rescue some of the greatest of these names from oblivion, and to give to Henry Yevele some small part of the recognition he deserves.

It will certainly be asked: where is Yevele to be ranked in the hierarchy of great artists and great men? This inevitable question is ultimately un-answerable, and as usual it demands the comparison of incomparables. How is it possible to determine, except by personal opinion, the relative rank of Imhotep of the Third Dynasty of Egypt; Ictinus and Callicrates in Periclean

Athens; Deinocrates of Ephesus; the Emperor Hadrian; Pierre de Montreuil, architect to St. Louis; Giotto; Sinan the Albanian, the servant of Soliman the Magnificent; Michelangelo; Sir Christopher Wren? What is certain is that it is among these names of the very greatest architects that that of Henry Yevele belongs. I have already compared his work for English architecture with the formation of English language and literature by Chaucer, and there is nothing far-fetched in this comparison, but just as Chaucer has a significance which far transcends national boundaries, so has Yevele in his own medium, which by its nature requires no translation and but little explanation.

It is precisely in the international significance of art that a great danger lies, as well as the secret of art's humanising influence. It is, or should be, obvious that the true artist is concerned in the first place with his art, and not with nationality; there is something ridiculous and even terrifying about the earnest nationalists who quote "Sumer is icumen in" as a proof of English musical superiority to the Continent, or of Poles or Czechs who place Chopin or Dvorak on pedestals as national heroes rather than as composers. England has in the past suffered through being imbued with a contrary spirit; notwithstanding an ebullient hatred of foreigners we absorbed the sculpture of Torrigiano, the painting of Holbein, Van Dyck, and Lely, the music of Handel and Mendelssohn; eventually London became so much the refuge of all artists (even self-styled ones) unable to live in their own countries, that the native artists began to be in actual want and to disappear altogether. This has led to an error just as damnable as the nationalistic one: namely the slothful cosmopolitan attitude of "why should we worry; if someone else can do the job better, don't let's bother."

From this attitude comes the appalling monotony of so much "modernist" architecture; instead of being designed by natives with a background of traditional materials and methods, it is machine-made for supply in standard patterns to every country on earth. It is based on the assumption that the essential requirements of all human beings are alike, regardless of class, nationality, climate, or tradition. This is a tragic fallacy, whose futility has been often enough demonstrated in the political and religious spheres of life. The most precious thing in human life is the spark of individuality and conscious discrimination which can be exerted—the living and moving pattern formed by what has been termed Free Will. Like all great men, Yevele can be distinguished by his immense individuality, and superimposed on this, by his belonging to England while at the same time he belongs to the human race, just as Bach, the supreme exponent of the world's abstract music, is at the same time German.

If any good can come from studying such a life as Yevele's, buried beneath half a millennium of events, it should be this: to see the problems which were dealt with, free from passion and partisanship, and to appreciate the solutions discovered by a great human mind. Thus the knowledge, poise, and taste acquired by Yevele in the course of a long and fruitful life may not be lost with his earthly existence, but transmuted by the vitality of living men will become truly immortal.

APPENDIX
PORTRAITS OF HENRY YEVELE

IT IS WELL KNOWN THAT PORTRAIT HEADS OF CRAFTSMEN ARE OFTEN FOUND carved in stone and wood in mediaeval buildings, and at Winchester College figures of the master mason, carpenter, and glazier, with the Clerk of the Works, are found in the stained glass put up in 1393 (48).

A master craftsman of such importance as Henry Yevele must have appeared at some of his many works, and it is practically certain that one of the label-stops of the arch leading from the Westminster Cloister entry to the courtyard of the Abbot's House (Deanery) was intended as his portrait, corresponding to Abbot Litlyngton on the other side, and forming one of a series with heads of Edward III and Queen Philippa and of the Black Prince and his wife Joan, in the Cloister entry itself. Unfortunately this label-stop is greatly decayed, and is useless as an indication of Yevele's features.

Roughly contemporary with this work was the new choir of the Hospital of St. Katharine-by-the-Tower, built at Queen Philippa's expense between 1351 and her death in 1369. The building itself has gone, but the stalls of c. 1365 remain. Among the misericord carvings is the head of a man wearing the round cap usually associated with the master of the works; it is clearly intended as a portrait, and shows a strong face with wrinkled forehead, firm nose, prominent cheek-bones, long, thick, curling hair, forked beard, and curling moustaches springing from below the nostrils, leaving the upper lip clean shaven. From the detail of the stalls, there can be little doubt that they were made by the royal craftsmen, of whom Yevele had been the chief since 1360. The elbows of the two corner stalls bear good portraits of Edward III and Queen Philippa herself. There is then some reason for thinking that this craftsman's head is that of Yevele (Title vignette).

Thirdly, there is a remarkable head of an old man on one of the bosses of the east walk of the Cloisters at Canterbury Cathedral. My attention was drawn to this boss by Mrs. Dorothy Gardiner, who first suggested that it might be a portrait of Yevele. It shows the face of an aged man surrounded with abundant curling hair and beard, and moustaches of the same form as those of the St. Katharine's head. The wrinkled forehead, nose, cheekbones, and form of the brows are also closely similar. The eyes of the Canterbury head are closed, and this must indicate that the subject was dead when the boss was carved, some time shortly after 1400 (40).

The handling of the face is of exquisite tenderness, and I believe could only have been achieved by a carver who had known and deeply loved his subject, and had felt for him the same affection which caused Thomas Occleve to have Chaucer's portrait painted "to putte othir men in remembraunce of his persone." Possibly the carver was Stephen Lote, or some other pupil of Yevele's. There is no means of reaching certainty, and it is open to everyone to reach his own conclusions, but for me this Canterbury head more than fulfils the ideal portrait of Yevele previously wrought by my own imagination.

BIBLIOGRAPHY

References for the known facts of the life of Henry Yevele are to be found in:

D. Knoop and G. P. Jones: *An Introduction to Freemasonry;* 1937. Henry Yevele and his Associates, in the *Journal* of the Royal Institute of British Architects, 25 May, 1935.

Exceptions to this are his work for the Abbot of Westminster at Chelmsford in 1372, recorded in the Abbey Muniments (No. 19866) quoted by E. Jervoise in *Ancient Bridges of Mid- and Eastern England,* 1932; and the facts concerning the nave of Canterbury Cathedral, detailed by Arthur Oswald in the *Burlington Magazine,* December, 1939.

The *Calendar of Close Rolls,* 1405–9, p. 88, recites the deed of 29 July, 1398 to which Yevele and Lote were witnesses at Wennington; Robert Yevele is mentioned in rolls at the Public Record Office, E.101/472/10 and 12, and in *Cal. Close Rolls,* 1441–47, pp. 480–82, where the descent of some of Henry Yevele's Southwark properties is given in enrolled deeds; see also pp. 236, 439, 447; and *Cals. Close Rolls,* 1435–41, p. 482, and 1399–1402, p. 154, which last reports the result of the inquisition held before the escheator for Kent concerning Yevele's life grant of the manors of Tremworth and Vannes. This inquisition also gives the exact date of his death. References to property transactions in which Yevele was concerned occur in the Surrey Feet of Fines (*Surrey Archaeological Society,* extra vol. 1894), pp. 145, 154, and in the MS. Calendars of Bridge House Deeds (Corporation of London), *passim.* His presence at Farnham in 1381 is attested by a document printed in *Crondal Records* (Hants. Record Society, 1891), p. 42.

Master John Box's work at Queenborough Castle is referred to in *Cals. Patent Rolls,* 1361–64, p. 430, and 1367–70, p. 238, and I owe to the kindness of Professor Douglas Knoop extracts relating to this work from a P.R.O. account, E.101/483/25.

A life of Yevele by Professor A. F. Pollard appears in the *Dictionary of National Biography,* and the accounts of Yevele and his contemporaries in the late Professor W. R. Lethaby's *Westminster Abbey and the King's Craftsmen,* 1906, and *Westminster Abbey Re-examined,* 1925, should also be read by every student of the period.

The "Articles and Points of Masonry" are printed from the two earliest versions (late fourteenth and early fifteenth century) in D. Knoop and G. P. Jones: *The Mediaeval Mason,* 1933, pp. 261–271.

Apart from matters of general history, references for most of the remaining material will be found in my article *The Mediaeval Office of Works,* in the *Journal* of the British Archaeological Association, 3rd Series, Vol. VI, 1941; in *The Mediaeval Carpenter* in *Journal* R.I.B.A., 13 June 1938; in *Henry Yevele, Architect, and His works in Kent,* in *Archaeologia Cantiana,* LVI, 1944; and in *The Education of the Mediaeval Architect,* in *Journal* R.I.B.A., June 1945.

HENRY YEVELE'S WORKS IN ARCHITECTURE

A CHRONOLOGICAL TABLE

Works certainly ascribed are shown in capitals; if doubtful, in lower case type; destroyed works are in italics.

DOMESTIC AND CIVIC

1358	*KENNINGTON MANOR (part)*	1372	*CHELMSFORD: MOULSHAM*
1362	WESTMINSTER: ABBOT'S		*BRIDGE*
	HOUSE, &c.	1376	*LONDON: SAVOY PALACE (part)*
1365	*WESTMINSTER: PALACE CLOCK*	1380	Arundel College
	TOWER	1383	*ROCHESTER BRIDGE*
?	*LONDON BRIDGE (parts)*	1389	*LONDON: TOWER WHARF*
1370	Cobham College, Kent	1395	WESTMINSTER HALL

MILITARY

			Arundel Castle: Great Hall, &c.
1361	*Queenborough Castle*	1383	Saltwood Castle
	LONDON: TOWER; BLOODY	1385	CANTERBURY: CITY WALLS
	TOWER, &c.		Bodiam Castle [(parts)
1378	CANTERBURY: WEST GATE	1390	*WINCHESTER CASTLE (repairs)*
1380	*THAMES DEFENCE TOWERS*		*CANTERBURY CASTLE (repairs)*
	COWLING CASTLE		

ECCLESIASTICAL

1351	*London: St. Katharine's-by-the-Tower*
1352	Westminster Abbey: South Cloister
1362	WESTMINSTER ABBEY: NAVE AND WEST CLOISTER
1363	Canterbury Cathedral: Black Prince's Chantry
1370	Cobham Church, Kent: tower, &c.
1371	LONDON CHARTERHOUSE
1377	CANTERBURY CATHEDRAL: NAVE (First Work)
1379	*BATTERSEA CHURCH: EAST WINDOW*
1380	Arundel Collegiate Church
1381	LONDON: ST. DUNSTAN IN THE EAST (South aisle and Porch)
1384	*London Bridge: St. Thomas's Chapel*
1391	CANTERBURY CATHEDRAL: NAVE (Second Work)
?	Meopham Church (New Work)
1395	Maidstone Church and College

MONUMENTAL

1360	*London: St. Paul's: Tomb of Sir John Beauchamp*
1370	Cobham Church, Kent: Sedilia, &c.
1372	London: Charterhouse; Tomb of Sir Walter Manny
1373	Lewes Priory (now Chichester Cathedral): Tombs for Earl and Countess of Arundel
1374	*LONDON: ST. PAUL'S; TOMB OF JOHN OF GAUNT*
1376	Canterbury Cathedral: Tomb of the Black Prince
1377	WESTMINSTER ABBEY: TOMB OF EDWARD III
1379	Durham Cathedral: Neville Screen
?	Selby Abbey: Sedilia
1380	Arundel Church: Pulpit
1389	WESTMINSTER ABBEY: TOMB OF CARDINAL LANGHAM
	London: St. Paul's; Tomb of Sir Simon Burley
1395	WESTMINSTER ABBEY: TOMB OF RICHARD II AND ANNE
?	London: St. Bartholomew the Great; Tomb of Rahere

PEDIGREE OF YEVELE, Etc.

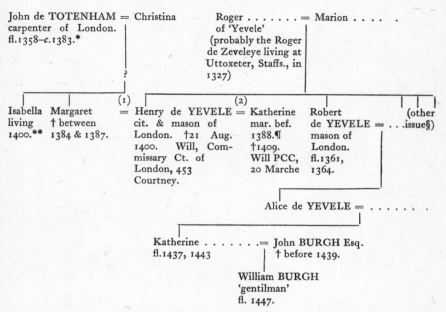

John de TOTENHAM = Christina   Roger . . . . = Marion . . . . .
carpenter of London. |
fl.1358–c.1383.*   of 'Yevele'
                       (probably the Roger
                       de Zeveleye living at
                       Uttoxeter, Staffs., in
                       1327)

          ?

Isabella   Margaret   (1)   (2)   Katherine   Robert   (other
living   † between   = Henry de YEVELE = Katherine   de YEVELE = . . .issue§)
1400.**   1384 & 1387.   cit. & mason of   mar. bef.   mason of
                     London. †21 Aug.   1388.¶   London.
                     1400.   Will, Com-   †1409.   fl.1361,
                     missary Ct. of   Will PCC,   1364.
                     London, 453   20 Marche
                     Courtney.

                                Alice de YEVELE = ...

             Katherine . . . .= John BURGH Esq.
             fl.1437, 1443   † before 1439.

                     William BURGH
                     'gentilman'
                     fl. 1447.

* The parentage of Margaret and Isabella is made almost certain by the reference in a deed of 20 April 1383 (B.M. Harl. Ch. 58 D.30) to the possibility of Margaret asking her dower of a tenement with four shops, etc., once belonging to John Tudenham, carpenter. From several other documents it is clear that this property was identical with that described in the register of quit-rents of Bridge House properties in 1358–9 (Bridge House Deeds, S.R., 76d.): "In the parish of St. Martin Otiswyche—A tenement belonging to John de Totenham, with four shops thereto annexed on the North, and five on the South, situated between the tenement sometime belonging to William de Caustone on the South and the church of St. Martin aforesaid on the North, and Bisschopisgatestrete on the East. 3s." A marginal note reads "merchanttaillors."

§ Henry Yevele's will refers to deceased brothers and sisters.

¶ Katherine had previously been the wife of John Hadde:

           Katherine . . . . = John HADDE, alias "Lightfoot"
           (afterwards second wife | of London. †before 1388.
           Henry Yevele)

           John HADDE   Elizabeth HADDE = William
           † s.p. c.1390   KYRTON

** Isabella was in 1383 the wife of William PALMER, citizen and horse-dealer of London, who died before 1400.

Authorities: J. G. Nichols in *London & Middlesex Archaeological Society's Transactions*, ii, 259–266; *Cal. Close Rolls*, 1399–1402, p. 154; 1441–47, pp. 480–482; W. J. Hardy and W. Page: Feet of Fines, London and Middlesex, p. 144; and see bibliography.

INDEX

The numerals in heavy type refer to the figure numbers of illustrations